PROFITING

WITH

IRON
CONDOR
OPTIONS

STRATEGIES FROM THE
FRONTLINE FOR TRADING IN
UP OR DOWN MARKETS

MICHAEL HANANIA
BENKLIFA

Vice President, Publisher: Tim Moore
Associate Publisher and Director of Marketing: Amy Neidlinger
Executive Editor: Jim Boyd
Editorial Assistant: Pamela Boland
Development Editor: Russ Hall
Operations Manager: Gina Kanouse
Senior Marketing Manager: Julie Phifer
Publicity Manager: Laura Czaja
Assistant Marketing Manager: Megan Colvin
Cover Designer: Chuti Prasertsith
Managing Editor: Kristy Hart
Project Editor: Anne Goebel
Copy Editor: Cheri Clark
Proofreader: Linda Seifert
Indexer: Lisa Stumpf
Compositor: TnT Design, Inc.
Manufacturing Buyer: Dan Uhrig

© 2011 by Pearson Education, Inc.
Publishing as FT Press
Upper Saddle River, New Jersey 07458

FT Press offers excellent discounts on this book when ordered in quantity for bulk purchases or special sales. For more information, please contact U.S. Corporate and Government Sales, 1-800-382-3419, corpsales@pearsontechgroup.com. For sales outside the U.S., please contact International Sales at international@pearson.com.

Printed in the United States of America

Second Printing: March 2012

ISBN-10: 0-13-439460-7
ISBN-13: 978-0-13-439460-2

Pearson Education LTD.
Pearson Education Australia PTY, Limited.
Pearson Education Singapore, Pte. Ltd.
Pearson Education Asia, Ltd.
Pearson Education Canada, Ltd.
Pearson Educatión de Mexico, S.A. de C.V.
Pearson Education—Japan
Pearson Education Malaysia, Pte. Ltd.
Library of Congress Cataloging-in-Publication Data is on file.

This product is printed digitally on demand. This book is the paperback version of an original hardcover book.

Pour ma mère,
For my beautiful wife Adira,
and for my wonderful children
Yehudah, Shimon, Chana, and Chaim

Table of Contents

Foreword

Option traders have an advantage over other investors because they can structure positions that generate a profit regardless of the direction of movement of the underlying security. Many of these trades generate their maximum profit if the underlying stock remains motionless for an extended period of time. Condor is such a trade. Simply stated, condors generate large profits when the underlying security remains range-bound for the duration of the trade. Properly structured condors can absorb large market changes and still generate impressive profits.

This characteristic has made condors one of the most popular trades among knowledgeable investors who have discovered the benefits of not betting on the direction of anything. Their view is exactly opposite that of a stock picker who spends all his time searching for "underpriced" securities that can be purchased below fair value. Condor traders assume that the market knows the fair value of a stock or index, and that it will continue to trade close to the current price until additional news generates a distinctly different view. Moreover, because option prices are based on volatility, they normally comprehend the effects of such news. A knowledgeable option trader, therefore, should be able to structure profitable condors in most markets.

As always, the devil is in the details. If structuring profitable condors was easy, everyone would be rich; there would be nothing to write about, and this book would collapse into a single page with a bulleted list of rules. But nothing could be further from the truth. Condors have four moving parts that are each affected by time and volatility. Volatility, in turn, has a structure that varies according to strike price and expiration date. It often rises or falls in a complex pattern that can be difficult to understand. Writing these words causes me to remember a conversation with Michael where he pointed out that the trade is somewhat asymmetrical because volatility falls in a rising market but rises in a falling market. Adjustments on the call side should, therefore, be handled differently than adjustments on the put side. That little nugget of gold and its associated details are just one of hundreds contained in this book.

Just a few years ago, private investors could dabble in the market and still make money. Those days are gone forever. Today's complex markets are a challenge for even the most sophisticated investor. Successful trading strategies are built around complex trade structures, careful risk management, a detailed understanding of how the market responds to news and events, and precise timing. This book explores all those topics and more for one of the most popular trade structures. More importantly, it represents the accumulated knowledge of many years of trading with millions of dollars in one of the most turbulent markets in history.

—**Jeff Augen**
Author of *Trading Options at Expiration*
December 2010

Acknowledgments

First, I'd like to thank my Creator who makes all things possible. I never forget (Devarim 8:11-18).

A book like this happens because many people along the way helped me get to where I am. I want to thank David Goldberg, Joseph Benporat, and Shelly Rosenberg for opening the door and helping me get through it. Oscar Rosenberg, Fred Todd, Miky Goldschmiedt, Susan Diamond, and David Schwarcz for having faith and confidence in my abilities and, literally, pushing me into this. Thanks, Susan, for all the opinions, ideas, articles, and support. Steve Lentz for always being there to answer the tough questions. Frank Fahey for his insights and direction. Alex Lushtak and Anatoly Tikhman for giving me a chance. Gene Lushtak who still can explain what I do better than I can. To my wonderful in-laws Steve and Carolyn Kayne for being the perfect "average investors" for me to test my ideas. Jim Boyd at FT Press who actually understands options and for giving me this opportunity. Michael Thomsett for doing a fantastic editing job and saving me from myself.

David Lehrfield for great execution of trades, for disagreeing with me constantly, and for being a great friend. You'll find a lot of you in this book.

I'd especially like to thank my Options Guru, Jeff Augen, on a number of levels. Not only would this book have not come to fruition without his direct involvement, but he profoundly changed the way I think and approach options as a trader. Read his books and be transformed. I look forward to the day when you ring the bell.

Finally, without the patience and encouragement of my wife Adira and my kids Yehudah, Shimon, Chana, and Chaim, I never would have finished the book.

Thanks one and all!

About the Author

Michael Hanania Benklifa manages millions of dollars worth of condor trades every month for private investors through his firm, Othello Consulting. He formerly served as a Financial Advisor for UBS and as an M&A Analyst for several large pharmaceutical companies. Benklifa holds an MBA from Texas A&M, as well as a Diplôme (Masters in Management) from École Supérieure de Commerce in France, and a BA in Philosophy from the University of Texas.

Preface

I used to hate trading. The problem with stock trading is that you have to know too much in order to be correct, or you have to trade on blind faith. People buy and sell stock every day without having the slightest idea about the company or the stock they are trading.

A while back I used to work in Mergers and Acquisitions. My job was to determine the viability of businesses for acquisition by large corporations. Let's scale it down and say you have $100,000 and you want to buy a small business. What kinds of things do you want to know about that business? You need to look at the books and track revenues, profits, and expenses. But to buy a business solely on that information would be foolish.

You also want to know about the competition, market share, number of competitors, and competitive advantage. Without an understanding of the competitors and who they are, you don't really have a grasp of the future of the company.

There's more. Who are the suppliers? What contracts exist? Who else do they supply? The supply line is crucial for the bottom line.

There are even more questions about the employees. You need to know who is indispensable and who isn't and what kind of employment contracts are in place. You need to talk to the sales staff and marketing department to get their perspective.

There are many more questions you should ask about a business before investing. Yet almost everybody who invests in stocks cannot answer the most basic questions about a company. Pick your favorite company. Can you name its five biggest competitors? How about the main suppliers? Would you buy a business by just looking at charts? Usually just those few questions are enough to stop people cold. Still, people will put their life savings on a name about which they really know nothing.

Who actually knows the answers to those questions? Maybe there are things about the company that full-time experts know and that you never will know. Even those experts still will get it wrong some of the time.

So I hated trading because I didn't believe I had the confidence to make sound decisions that wouldn't just be guesses at the end of the day. I was a Financial Advisor and people were always asking me about what I thought about the market or whether I had a good stock tip. It wasn't too impressive to say, "I don't know," but it was an honest answer. I mostly recommended Structured Products, hybrids of stocks, options, and bonds designed for hedging risk. Some of those Structured Products were unfortunately issued and guaranteed by venerable institutions like Lehman Brothers. The more I learned about these products, the more I started to learn about the intricacies of options.

What appealed to me about options was that there were strategies that worked even if you didn't know anything about the company whatsoever. You didn't even need to know whether the price was going to go up or down. In fact, the trade had nothing to do with either the company or the price. It had to do with the fear built into the price and how much time was left until expiration. The actual ticker was irrelevant. So now I realized I could trade without having an opinion.

Over time, I worked on and studied various options strategies and adopted condors as my favorite. There are a number of ways to trade this strategy and I tried them all. The strategy presented in this book is the one that I find works best in a variety of market conditions. In the very difficult market conditions of the past few years, I've managed to generate pretty decent returns on a regular basis. Don't be surprised if your returns are in the 30% to 60% range in a year. No guarantees, but it can be done.

There are a few questions I'm always asked after I explain what I do. The first is always, "What's the risk?" The second is, "Why have I never heard about this before?" The third is, "Why doesn't everybody do this?"

As to the first question, I always describe the risky nature of the trade. There is a lot of risk in this trade. Everybody should consider the nature of the trade and how much they are willing to risk and who they are willing to risk it with. Results count. I'm generally far more risk averse than I am for the clients whose capital I trade.

"Why have I never heard about this before?" The answer to this question is not so simple. The ordinary investor either is trading his own stocks or has handed a portfolio over to an advisor to manage for him.

Advisors by and large don't really want anything to do with options. What they do understand about options is generally very limited, and their approach is pretty simple. They trade them like stocks. Buy this or that option and see what happens at expiration. The other officially condoned strategy is covered calls. Additionally, my experience at large firms is that they actually dissuade advisors from trading options in any sophisticated manner. There are generally no tools on the system to do proper analysis of options even if they wanted to trade effectively. I was told by a chief options strategist at a major brokerage that they don't want their advisors trading options because they are worried about big mistakes. That is a smart decision on their part but truly limits what you as a trader and investor can do to earn money and protect your assets.

Additionally, sophisticated option trades require constant supervision. An easy trade needs no attention, but you can never tell which one is an easy trade until you are done. Markets can move on a dime and you have to be ready to respond. Unless you have the luxury to pay attention to the market and place orders when necessary, you could increase your risk in a trade substantially.

The last question is, "Why doesn't everybody do this?" This has a few different answers. First is the poor experience investors have had with options in the past. Most of those burned by options have lost money buying options, which is all too often a sucker's bet. Second is a genuine lack of education and understanding of options and particular strategies, which this book seeks to help remedy. The third answer is that no one will do this job for you. Your advisor will not manage options strategies for you because there is not enough money in this for him relative to the risk involved. He will not monitor it because he has 100 other clients for which he has to make financial plans. Mutual funds don't do this because it's not in their charter. Hedge funds are too big. They can't just step up and start spending a billion dollars in the options market.

Many people have asked me why I'm giving away my strategy. They wonder, wouldn't that ruin its effectiveness? First of all, I didn't invent condors nor am I reinventing the wheel. This is a merely a strategy and not a formula. Think of it as a method or an approach to trading condors. What's missing for a lot of traders or people who would like to trade options is a proper understanding of how options really work. There are a lot of moving parts to track. I imagine stock trading akin to flipping a coin. Options trading is more like playing chess.

Two caveats before going forward:

> **Caveat #1:** By their very nature, condors are high-risk strategies. They can blow up on you and you can lose all or most of the money you put up in the trade. This book takes that possibility into account and points out ways to diminish but not eliminate the risk. You will learn that picking the right instrument to trade, picking the size of your condor, strategically choosing your entry and exit points, limiting your time in the market and, especially, not getting greedy will all help to mitigate risk. But there is always the possibility of total failure regardless of all the risk management in the world.

Caveat #2: This is not an income strategy. In order to entice people to attend classes or buy books, many people would call this an income-generating strategy because of how successful it can be on a regular basis. But calling this an income strategy is misleading and inaccurate.

An options condor is a trade. That's it. No more and no less. If you start thinking of this as an income strategy or, worse still, depending on it for your income, you will lose all of it. You will push this strategy too far and too hard and the condor will swoop down and eat you alive.

Caveats aside, I absolutely love trading condors. I've made a lot of money for myself and my clients even though I've also had many sleepless nights. However, making money is never easy and never without risk. Still, there is a certain pride about making stellar returns even when I am wrong about market direction.

A condor is a big bird with a wingspan that can reach 10 feet. When it flies, it flaps only occasionally and glides most of the way. The silent, patient image of this lovely bird floating through time and space will provide a useful metaphor for the trade you will learn. Like the flapping of its wings, the opening and closing of a condor trade should be done infrequently. The patient drift through calm air reflects the slow and steady time decay and the low volatility that will lift our profits. Treat this awesome bird with the respect it deserves and you can ride on its wings.

Chapter 1

The Horse Race

An iron condor is a complex options trade that creates a "zone," as illustrated in Figure 1.1, in which a profit occurs over time and within a specific price range. Correctly picking the direction of price movement is not necessary. Understanding the dynamics involved in the trade is the key to long-term success and limited risk.

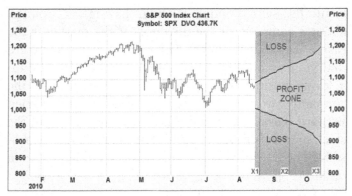

Source: OptionVue 6

FIGURE 1.1   *S&P 500 Index chart*

Too Good to Be True

Too many people trade options without knowing about the range of risks they face, or without first acquiring the knowledge they need. This book addresses that problem with respect to condor trading. Nonetheless, condors are lucrative and you can create profits quite easily; but you can also lose money in a condor trade. Condors are the most consistently profitable trade you can create, with potential annual returns reaching 30%, 40%, 50%, or more if put together correctly.

Just as there are different ways to play chess, there are different strategic methods for trading options. This book presents a conservative strategy designed to maximize gains and minimize risk.

Introduction to Trading

Ironically, with condor trading, having an opinion about a company or the direction of the market is the easiest way to lose money. The more convinced you are that your opinion is correct, the more you'll hold onto a losing position and ignore the realities, not of the company but of your trade. A wise investor named Bernard Baruch once said that the main purpose of the stock market is to make fools of as many people as possible. The best response to this advice is to not have an opinion.

There are very few places where not having an opinion is actually profitable, and surprisingly the options world is one of those places. Some options strategies are "market neutral," meaning their potential to generate a profit is not dependent on whether the market goes up or down. Actually, these market-neutral strategies do best when the market moves up *and* down within a given timeframe.

Once upon a time, a myth was perpetuated that all you had to do was keep your money in the stock market and you would get rich and retire. This assumption was considered so obvious that something called an "Individual Retirement Account," or IRA, was created so that people could put their money in the stock market and benefit from tax incentives. The fundamental problem with this way of thinking is that people forgot that the stock market is a place of investment with all of its associated risks and dangers. It is *not* a retirement account. After the 2008–09 crash in the market, most people are now painfully aware of this fact. The buy-and-hold strategy is *not* guaranteed to create wealth.

Investing also presents you with a huge obstacle, namely, acquiring and applying knowledge. Do you really know more than the stock market? If Apple is priced at $200, you need to know something that nobody else knows in order to believe that the market has mispriced Apple and that the company should be worth either much more or much less. Actually convincing yourself that you have an edge against full-time professionals with their massive supercomputers and their team of Ph.D. programmers is delusional. Chances are if you do make money investing in the market, you are likely riding the wave that is making everybody else money as well—in other words, you got lucky!

There is another way to make money in the stock market that has nothing whatsoever to do with investing: *trading*. Investing requires, or at least should require, research, understanding, careful analysis, and strategy regarding a company and its sector. Trading is simply about making money. The shorter the timeframe involved in the trade, the less significant fundamental information and all the accompanying research becomes.

Swing traders like to trade in a timeframe of days or weeks. Day traders like to trade in a timeframe of hours or minutes or even seconds. Now computers are involved in high-frequency trading (HFT), which moves money in and out of positions in millionths of a second. Computers have taken any kind of qualitative edge away from human traders. They can process all relevant news and information and trade accordingly before the nerves in your eyes can electrically send the visual information of the words you just read to your brain.

There is one domain where computers will not drive out the human competition. That is the world of options trading. Options traders observe and rely on the market's emotions, fear, and panic, and design their moves to maximize or minimize the effects of time. Increased fear means increased prices in options, and decreased fear means lower prices. Although computers have been programmed to exploit mispriced options in an instant, fear is something computers don't understand...yet.

How Options Work

Options can be thought of as the Swiss Army knife of trading. The combinations and maneuvers available in options trading strategies seem endless. By comparison, stock trading is a simple directional trade. The decision to buy or sell a stock is usually done through fundamental analysis or technical charting techniques. Options traders look at these tools and so much more.

This section is not meant to be an introduction to options, but rather an introduction to options *trading*. Most options books focus a great deal on comparing completely different options strategies and on what happens at the *end* of an options trade. A skilled options trader, however, might be in and out of the trade several times before expiration.

In this book the focus is more on practical trading strategies and less on theory. It's not what you know, it's "how" you know it. Your significant paradigm shift is to think like traders and not like investors.

Summarizing some of the basics of options trading is a good starting point for the following review. This review is not meant to be comprehensive but, rather, to serve as an *approach* that shows you what you need to know in order to get going. Even if you already have some ideas about how options work, the following discussion might still give you food for thought.

The Horse Race

The following analogy gives you a mind-set for options trading. Picture a horse race in which you place your bet. The value of your bet depends on the odds. If your horse is a 2-1 favorite, your chances of winning are high but you won't make much money. If the horse you pick is 100-1, your chances of winning are remote but if you do win the payout will be huge.

So you go to the horse race and you bet on your favorite horse, SeeBo, who is rated at 100-1, to win. The race is four laps, and as it begins you wait to see whether you will win or lose at the end. Pretty straightforward so far.

Now add a twist to make this race more interesting. You can buy or sell your bet *during* the race. If you are the kind of person who just likes to wait until the end of the race, then this twist changes nothing. If you are the kind who likes to take advantage of a positive development or if you are risk averse, this new dynamic changes everything, making it literally a whole new horse race.

Run through the possibilities to get a better picture of the complexities this twist adds.

First Lap

After the first lap, SeeBo, surprisingly, is in the lead. You hold a bet in your hand that could be worth a fortune if SeeBo keeps this up and wins the race. What do you do? Do you sell it now? There are still three laps to go, so you won't get as much for your bet now as you would in the end—but is a little profit better than nothing? You decide to hold on.

Second Lap

In the second lap SeeBo fades and starts to fall behind. You regret not selling the bet when you had a chance, but still, if you sell it now you might get some of your money back. Instead you decide to hold on because you believe he really "should" win.

Third Lap

Third lap and SeeBo has caught his second wind, now starting to close in on first place. You pat yourself on the back for your intelligence since you were obviously right. The bet is gaining in value, so why sell it now when you could win big?

Final Stretch

Final stretch, and your heart is beating fast. What is your bet worth if SeeBo is way in front? What if SeeBo is neck and neck? What if he starts to fall behind? Time is running out quickly and his position now is absolutely critical because there is almost no time for major changes in the outcome.

And the Winner Is...

It doesn't matter because now you get the idea. In a nutshell these are the kinds of dynamics involved in options trading. Just as the horse race has a finish line, options have an expiration date, the third Friday (for index options) or Saturday (for equity options) of every month, at which point either they have value or they don't. Prior to that date, the value changes based on the changing odds, being in-the-money or out-of-the-money, and the time remaining until expiration.

The energy and excitement of the race is expressed in different terms in options. The horse's position in the race is the Delta; so if your horse has a Delta of 1 he is way up front, and if he has a Delta of .1 then things are not looking so good. The speed with which he starts to catch up to first place is called Gamma. All the fear, hope, and energy of the race are expressed as Vega, also known as implied volatility. Of course, all of these concepts collapse when the race is over because all you have left is a winner or a loser.

When you buy an option, you are placing a very similar kind of bet to that of the horse race. If Apple is at $200 a share, you can place a $5 bet that it will rise to $220 during the next month. If in a month, Apple's price is $220 or more, the person who sold you the bet has to sell you Apple stock for $220. Unlike in the horse race, the potential profit is limitless because even if Apple stock goes to $300 the seller still has to sell you the stock at $220, and you get to make a cool $75 ($80 profit minus the $5 cost of the option) by reselling those same 100 shares of stock in the open market.

When you buy options and the price is in the winning zone, that option is "in-the-money." Buyers of options like to be in-the-money. Sellers would prefer that the price stay "out-of-the money."

Options are *not* investments. When you purchase options, you don't receive a dividend. You don't get annual reports or voting rights because you don't have a material interest in the company. When you buy options, all you receive are certain rights that you may choose to exercise.

For every buyer there is a seller, and you can be either. Selling options is also referred to as writing options because you are essentially "writing" a contract that obligates you to sell your options at the agreed price to the buyer at his discretion. In other words, you can think of an option contract as simply a promise, so options trading is merely the buying and selling of legally binding promises.

Just like the bookie in the horse race, the seller can profit only to the extent of the value of the initial bet, the sales price. The buyer is the one hoping to cash in big.

The flip side is that the buyer knows upfront how much he can lose, namely the money he paid for the option. The seller's potential loss may be unlimited if he sold a call, so his broker will require a certain amount of money to be available in order to pay in case of a big loss. This is the *margin* required to be kept on hand to protect the broker from catastrophic losses in case traders end up being wrong.

Those traders who buy calls want the market to go up, and those traders who buy puts want the market to go down. If you are a seller, you will lose money if the put you sell ends up in-the-money in the same way and proportion as if you had to pay for in-the-money call.

Buying Versus Selling

Which is better, to be a buyer or a seller? There are many factors that affect that decision, so there really is no "better." Both offer advantages and disadvantages.

The Buyer

The buyer has the advantage of potentially unlimited gains. He leverages his money through the purchase of options and can make returns several times his initial cost. He does, however, have a few things working against him.

Those who buy stocks have to get only one thing right: *direction*. If the stock goes up and they sell, they make money. Simple and uncomplicated. The buyer of options has to do the same thing, pick the right direction, but that's not all. He also has to be concerned with two additional factors: time and expiration.

Actually, picking the right direction is extremely difficult. An analyst who does nothing but study a certain company for years, talks to the CEO, knows the business inside and out, and even works at the company can still pick the wrong direction for the company's stock price. You, the ordinary investor, have access to no information that gives you an edge in the marketplace. Regardless, picking the correct direction is crucial for the stock buyer and also for the options buyer.

The options buyer can't just pick the right direction; he also has to pick the right distance the price will move. If he buys an option believing that Apple's stock price will go to $220, then Apple has to go to $220 and not just to $210. This is an example of getting the direction right but the distance wrong. Additionally, not only does the price of the stock have to reach $220, but the buyer also has to include the price of the option (for example, $5), which means the stock price has to go even further before he makes money. So you can be correct as to the strike price but can still make no money because you haven't covered your cost of purchasing the option.

Finally, the greatest difficulty the options buyer has to contend with is time. Correctly picking the direction and the strength of the move in that direction is worthless if the target is met after expiration day. If the market quickly moves favorably for the options buyer, there is a chance to make a profit if he quickly closes his trade. However, each day that goes by a little more value is lost in that option, making the likelihood of a profitable trade more remote if the stock doesn't do what the buyer hopes.

To review, the options buyer has to be correct about three things:

1. Direction

2. Distance

3. Time

All three have to be in confluence to create a profitable trade for the options buyer. Some simple odds demonstrate the difficulty in getting all three of these correct. Attribute 50/50 odds to correctly choosing each of the three elements. But 50/50 is generous. Direction is either up or down but distance and time are far more complicated. What do we get? Direction (50%) × Distance (50%) × Time (50%) = 12.5%. At best the odds of holding a profitable option at expiration are about 1 in 8. You may think you have an edge. Study after study shows you really don't.

The Seller

The seller of options has to be right about only one thing: *time*. He doesn't care if the direction works against him or even about the strength of the move. All he cares is that time works against the trade. At worst his odds are 50/50 because time will work either for him or against him. The disadvantage of selling is that if he is wrong about time, his losses could be potentially quite high.

From a risk/ratio perspective buying looks better than selling. You can lose only what you spent for the option, which is not a lot of money compared to buying 100 shares of stock. (Every option is equivalent to control over 100 shares.) The defined potential loss involved is why many people who go into options trading start by being buyers. The potential gain is unlimited. Nonetheless, the odds of a successful trade for a buyer are small. So even though the risk/reward profile is appealing, the odds of success are low.

The risk/reward of selling looks terrible. The gain is limited to the premium collected, and the potential for loss can be unlimited. To make selling more palatable, you want at least two things. First, you want to limit your potential loss, and second, you want to increase your odds of success as much as possible.

There are two ways to limit losses for a seller. The first and most popular way is to actually own the underlying stock when you sell calls (the popular "covered" call strategy). In a worst-case scenario the seller merely gives up the stock that he owns to the buyer if and when exercised, making a capital gain on the stock as well as keeping the option premium. The second way is to buy another option whose strike price is farther away from the option that was sold to cap the loss, creating what is called a "credit spread." A "spread" is the simultaneous opening of two or more option positions that offset each other in some manner. This can involve a long (buying) and short (selling) call or a long and short put; it can also involve variations in expiration date, strike price, or both. There are many kinds of spreads. The most important attribute of any spread is that it can reduce risk, even the risk of exercise. It can cap potential losses on the short side by an offsetting long position. The spread, specifically the credit spread, is the essence of the structure in a condor.

Think of a credit spread as simply "sell one and buy one." You make money on the one you sell, called the "short strike," but the potential loss can be unlimited. The option you buy, called the "long strike," is the one that makes you money when you pass the strike price. The difference between the two strikes is your maximum loss.

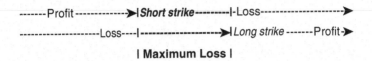

-------Profit-------------➤|*Short strike*---------|-Loss----------------------➤
---------------------Loss----|--------------------➤|*Long strike*-------Profit➤
| **Maximum Loss** |

A word on options quotes: Every quote is given in dollars and cents *per share* and without dollar signs. These translate to dollar value on a per-share basis; but options always relate to 100 shares, so the shorthand quotation has to be multiplied by 100. For example, an options quote of 1.50 equals $150.00 and a quote of 2.06 equals $206.00.

With this is mind, here's an example of applying the credit spread. Assume that Apple (AAPL) is currently at $200 a share. The price of a call at the 210 strike is 3.45 (that is, $345.00), which is the most the seller can make from selling one contract. The seller buys a 220 strike call for 1.41 ($141.00). So buying the call limits the potential loss to 2.05. If you do both—selling the 210 and buying the 220—you create a spread.

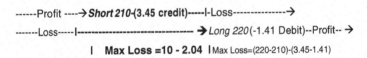

------Profit ----→ *Short 210*-(3.45 credit)-----|-Loss---------------→
-------Loss-----|---------------------------------- →*Long 220*(-1.41 Debit)--Profit-- →
| **Max Loss =10 - 2.04** | Max Loss=(220-210)-(3.45-1.41)

Figure 1.2 shows the same idea expressed graphically except here maximum loss doesn't consider the credit for the sale because we will only measure gain and loss relative to initial margin risk.

Source: OptionVue 6

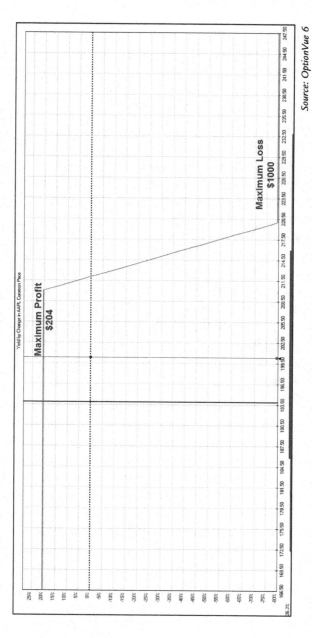

Source: OptionVue 6

FIGURE 1.2   *Yield by change in AAPL common price*

Figure 1.3 shows you what selling a spread on the call side looks like at expiration. You can also sell a spread on the put side that has the same profile, but with the price trend going in the other direction. Buying the outside strikes cuts the downward fall of the line and creates an outcome that looks like a wing. Two wings look like a bird and with that you have a condor.

For the ordinary stock trader there are a few counter-intuitive ideas that need digesting. First is the idea of selling as opposed to buying, especially regarding something you don't own. The second is that a strategy with a worse risk-to-reward ratio can be the better trade. Counterintuitive is not to be confused with contrarian. A contrarian wants to trade in the opposite direction of the trend of the market or stock because he thinks the masses are wrong. Counterintuitive trading says that the premises that seem logically correct on first blush might turn out to be exactly the wrong trade and the opposite approach is warranted. Even within condor trading you can employ a counterintuitive approach.

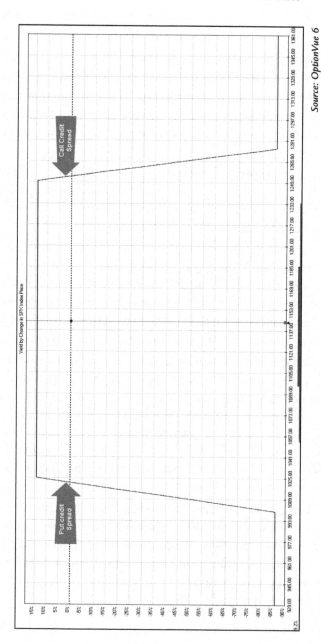

FIGURE 1.3   *Yield by change in SPX Index price*

Trading the Math

When you think back to the analogy of the horse race, you find a number of variables that affect the value of the bet before the end of the race. Time is a major consideration. Position during the race is crucial. But there are other elements of the race that affect the nature of the bet as well.

For example, acceleration changes everything. What if the horse bolts out of the gate far ahead of the pack? Suddenly the odds change dramatically in his favor. So you have to also keep track of acceleration.

How about other conditions that could change during the race? A sudden trip could break the horse's leg. It could start to rain. Lightning could spook the horses. The jockey could fall off. The possibilities go on and on. Depending on the severity of the change, you want some idea of how it affects your trade for better or worse.

What is the one consideration that seems to be gone from the picture? The horse itself. Maybe you picked the horse because you know horses. You grew up with horses. The jockey is your son. Maybe you picked the horse because, based on his past performance you think he is due to win. Whatever the reason you had for choosing the horse initially, it becomes irrelevant and superfluous once the race starts.

You are now playing the odds. The odds are set by the bookies and the other gamblers. You have to deal with that reality now. If you hold your ticket until the end of the race, that's one thing, but if you are trading during the race, you are trading the odds or, in other words, you are trading the math.

Options trading is ultimately all about trading the math. Once you are in a condor trade, you don't care about the market, the news, or the price direction—you care only about the math.

Trading stocks is also trading math but on a much simpler level. The reason that inspired you to buy a particular stock, whether it came through fundamental or technical analysis, takes a back seat to profit and loss. If your stock starts to lose too much money, you have to decide to stay in or get out. Your risk tolerance dictates your trade, not the stock. Your opinion about the company, the curves and indicators, all evaporate into nothing when you see the negative dollar signs getting larger and larger. You realize that the market doesn't care what you think or the price you paid for the stock. You now have to make a decision. Are you willing to lose $1 more or not? At this point you are trading math, period.

The same considerations occur when the stock goes up in value. Are you trying to capture a certain profit or are you just going to ride the trend or keep the stock through retirement? Here again, you are trading the math.

The nice thing about options is that all these considerations have been quantified and given names.

Time decay is called Theta. The effect of a change in price is called Delta. Acceleration is Gamma. Worry is expressed as Vega. The name for this group of "derivatives" is the Greeks.

In order to trade any options, it is useful to know how these work. For the topic of this book, you are interested only in how they affect condors. Knowing these risks and challenges in advance helps you get into a good trade. Keeping track of these risks and challenges during the trade helps you manage risk.

Time Is Money—Theta

Options trading requires you to reorient your thinking. When you're buying stock, the company behind the trade is important. Your goal is to be an informed and educated investor. But you are not investing when you buy and sell options—you are trading.

First and foremost, you are trading time. What does that mean? The longer the term of an option, the more time premium is built into its overall cost. An everyday example is the option period when you're buying a house. Tying up the house for one month will cost more than tying it up for one week. There is a cost to obligating the seller to remain committed to selling the house to you for a certain time and taking it off the market. Options are the same way. The longer the seller obligates himself, the more he will charge you.

A small amount is shaved off the price of an option every day. The rate and size of the depreciation is dependent on how close the contract is to expiration.

Picture a full pot of water costing $10. If you place a cold pot of water on a fire, the water slowly evaporates as it heats up. A half pot of water costs $5. The hotter the water, the quicker the evaporation, until there is no water left and the pot becomes worthless. Options mimic this curve of evaporation. It starts slowly and accelerates toward the end.

So you want to sell options when there is more time priced in, wait until the price evaporates somewhat, and then buy them to close and take your profit. *Sell high and buy low.* You are selling time at a high price and buying it to close at a lower price. The sequence of events when you *sell* is "sell-hold-buy," as opposed to the better-known long position's sequence, "buy-hold-sell."

So far you don't care about the underlying stock. You are looking for candidates that will move neither up nor down too much or too quickly, over a very short window of time. The alphabet soup of different ticker symbols is almost irrelevant. Some of the important considerations of the stock you pick include liquidity and volatility. What is not important is whether the fundamentals of the company are strong or weak. Charts are of limited value because they only tell you what has already happened. Almost everything a stock investor uses to weigh the decision is irrelevant when you sell condors.

Time decay doesn't appear to behave the same at all strike prices. The at-the-money (ATM) strike price decays differently than the out-of-the-money strike price. This difference is key for understanding entries and exits for the condor strategy.

Time decay accelerates quickly as expiration nears. So the best time to sell is as close to expiration as possible. Many condor traders like to sell about a month before expiration to take advantage of the accelerating time decay. Figure 1.4 represents the decay of at-the-money options 95 days out.

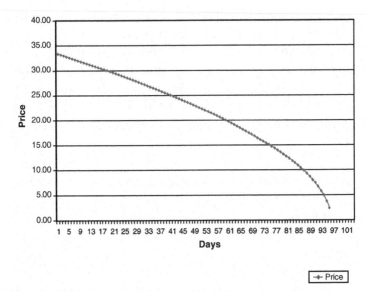

FIGURE 1.4   *Time decay at-the-money*

Out-of-the-money options have a very different profile. Their value drops dramatically and then levels off
close to expiration, reflecting the roller coaster of fear
(that is, implied volatility) and its interaction with the
more predictable decline in time value.

The reason to pick far out-of-the-money strikes is
their low exercise probability. If the price stays more or
less stable, those low probabilities cause the price to
drop quickly; as a seller, you want to see the value of the
premium drop as quickly as possible.

As shown in Figure 1.5, in the first 30 days, the value
went from approximately $1.60 to $0.80, a 50% drop.
In the next 15 days it lost another 50% to $0.40. Once
the option gets near zero in value, the curve simply flat-
tens out because there is almost no time value left to lose.

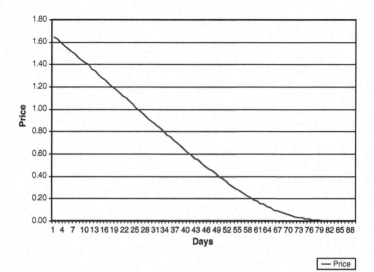

FIGURE 1.5   *Time decay out-of-the-money*

Time decay affects a condor's value just like all
option positions, and this is where you gain the edge.
Learning how to read and use the graph shown in
Figure 1.6 is crucial to your success as a condor trader.
The top line graph that looks like a condor is the value
at expiration and only at expiration. Your goal is not to
stay until expiration but to stay until you get the desired
return. So you need to know what your profit and loss
targets are *before* expiration. As time decay accumu-
lates, those levels change. The P&L curve for a condor
resembles an upside-down smile. Study the patterns of
the multiple curves.

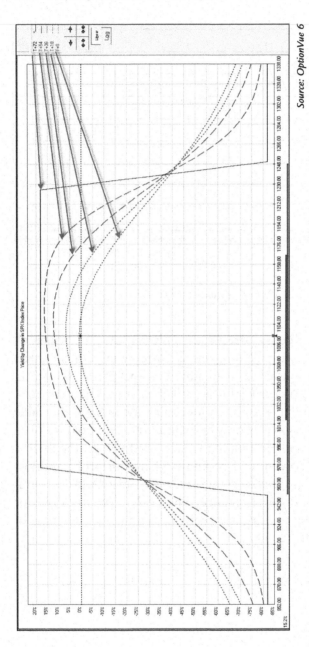

FIGURE 1.6   *Yield by change in SPX Index price*

In order to put on a strategy that sells for a credit, brokerages require that a certain amount of cash (or equivalent liquidity) be available in your account to cover against potential losses. Your "real" risk is the total potential loss minus the credit you received for selling the condor. So, for example, if your total potential loss is $10, the broker will require $10 to cover potential losses. However, because you received $2 in credit, your "real" risk is $8. However, in this book you need to look at the $10 only as your reference point because you are trying to measure your returns as a function of the cash you need to make available to do the trade. This condor, reflecting an actual trade, was sold for a 17% credit based on cash margin required.[1] The options expire in 72 days. The put strikes used were sell 975 and buy 950. The call strikes used were sell 1,225 and buy 1,250. The market was hovering at 1,100.

The first curve on the bottom represents the P&L from the day you entered the trade. The black dot represents the position value. If the price moved at all and traveled along the curve, the position would almost immediately lose value. Why? Remember, you are trying to make money from time decay. No time had elapsed yet so there was no accumulated value.

The second curve represents what should be the P&L 18 days from your entry. By the way, the 18 days includes the weekend. This model is theoretical because

---

1. *If one side of a condor requires a margin of $2,500 for a single contract condor with strikes 25 points apart then some brokerages will require an additional $2,500 as margin for the other side of the condor. Most options-savvy brokerages will allow you to margin the same $2,500 on both sides. Check with your broker to find out the policies used.*

it assumes no change in volatility over the period. This condor was sold at a 17% credit based on margin. After 18 days, if the market had remained right in the center, you were then able to give up 11% and keep 6%. You still had 54 days to expiration.

As time progressed, each curve broadened so the potential profit increased and the break-even points for the condor reached farther out. Decisions about exiting or adjusting the condor invariably have to be made considering the rate of time decay over the coming days and weeks. Remember, it is easy to get greedy and try to squeeze a little bit more money out of the condor, but decisions should rely on the risk/reward profile.

In a 72-day condor, for example, you might get 5% in 18 days. Those 18 days represent only 25% of the total length of the contract. If you wait 36 days, you could keep 12% of the 17%, which represents 71% of the total credit and 50% of the time of the total contract. Figure 1.7 proves that the best risk/reward ratio is halfway through the trade. There is a point where the risk/reward ratio shifts and, as the position moves closer to expiration, you start taking on ever higher risk to get each incremental percentage point.

You could decide to wait the entire 72 days with the idea of keeping the entire credit. But why? There are two truisms in the market. Truism #1: You can make money only if you are in the market. Truism #2: You can *lose* money only if you are in the market. If you are content with 6% (which is good by anybody's standard), why expose yourself to another 54 days of risk? Even if you want to stay 36 days and get 71% of the credit, why stay in the market for the remaining 29%?

Things go wrong and any great winning trade can start to lose money. Better to take the money off the table. Don't forget, you can always do another trade with contracts farther out in time. Another opportunity will eventually present itself.

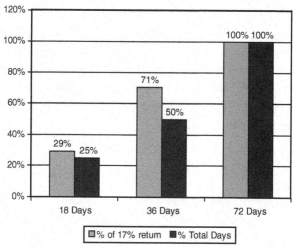

FIGURE 1.7   *Time risk versus reward*

Many who trade condors like to start the trade with 30 to 45 days until expiration because they believe that most of the time decay occurs in the last month. Although it is true that time decay accelerates in the last 1 to 2 weeks, no time is left for any kind of risk management besides simply closing the position and possibly taking a loss. Don't forget that for out-of-the-money options the greater decay happens very quickly and there is no need to hold the options until expiration.

One other consideration: Remember what you hope will happen. You want the underlying stock to remain stable for a period of time. How long seems reasonable? If you are in a condor trade and the market has been calm for a few weeks already, is it wise to assume that the market will stay calm? The caveat in trading is "don't push your luck."

So when you see a number next to Theta, that number represents the amount of value (theoretically) that will be lost in the option in one day. You also know that time decay for out-of-the-money options happens pretty quickly and that you don't need to stay in that long for a nice profit to be realized.

Volatility: Everything Else

The study of volatility is the subject of entire books and a slew of academic studies. You do need the foundation for a basic technical understanding of volatility and what it means in practice, but not the deep analysis that too often goes into its study.

Most of the elements that go into pricing an option are well known. You know the strike price, current price, current interest rates, dividends, and expiration date. There is no conjecture or debate about these. What's missing? Well, everything else. Every piece of information, conjecture, concern, and hope is the last piece that determines the price of an option. This piece is quantified and called implied volatility (IV).

Technically speaking, all of options trading can be understood as trading standard deviations. A standard deviation is a measure of the likelihood of a certain event happening. So if IV calculates a 1 standard deviation move from $90 to $110, then that means that there is a 68% chance that the price will fall in that range. In other words, there is a 34% chance it will move from 100 to 110 and a 34% chance it will move from 100 to 90, similarly depicted in Figure 1.8. Two standard deviations might be from $80 to $120, placing the odds of the price falling in that range to 95%. Three standard deviations place the odds at 98% that the price will fall between $70 and $130. Options trading is essentially trading a disagreement over standard deviations.

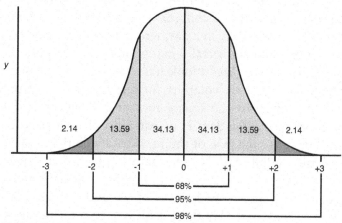

FIGURE 1.8   *Standard deviation curve*

For example, there are two traders with different views on a stock valued at $100. The calculation of IV currently predicts that a stock's 1 standard deviation move will be from $90 to $110. The put at 90 or the call at 110 will cost the buyer $10 ($1,000). The buyer disagrees with IV and believes that a 1 standard deviation will be greater than the $10 he paid. The buyer always thinks that the IV is lower than it should be and that he is getting a deal. The seller of the option must have the opposite opinion. For the seller, the IV is overpriced and that it reflects a 1 standard deviation move under $10. As such, if it moves $10 or more he loses money. Each is trading his prediction of a 1 standard deviation move versus the 1 standard deviation move priced into the option and expressed as IV. Just as in the stock market, for every buyer there is a seller, and each thinks the other is wrong.

So the implied volatility of an at-the-money call option is the market's collective prediction of how much a stock should move in a day, week, month, or year. The IV gives you a statistical window of what a 1 standard deviation move *should* look like. The way to calculate the projected stock volatility for one day is to take the IV and divide by the square root of 256, which is the number of trading days in a year. Since the square root of 256 is 16, the rule of thumb is to divide the implied volatility number by 16, and that will give you a 1 standard deviation move for one day. So if your implied volatility is 32%, divide 32% by 16 and you get 2%. Therefore, in one day there is a 68% chance the stock will make a 2% move. If you want to know how much the price could move on a different time scale, the formula is IV divided by 16 times the square root of the number of days in question. For example, if you want to know how much the price could move in 49 days, you take the square root of the number of 49, 7 in this case, and multiply your 2% against that number, which is 14%. Therefore, a volatility number of 32% is pricing in a 1 standard deviation range movement of 14% up or down over the next 49 days.

What is the practical implication of IV? After all is said and done, a higher IV means that options sell for a higher price than if IV were lower, and vice versa. IV gives you the probability of how far the market *should* move up or down in a given timeframe. However, the IV fluctuates constantly so it has limited predictive capability and usefulness. IV does not tell you what will happen next. This is important to remember. Like all indicators, IV works until it doesn't.

IV calculators easily show the odds of whether the trade should be profitable by a given date. Unfortunately, the use of probabilities frequently gives a false sense of security. You look at a trade that shows an 80% chance that the options will expire worthless and feel as though this is the easiest trade in the world. You should simply ignore the statistics or think of them as giving you a false sense of confidence. This is not to say the statistics are necessarily wrong; it is just safer to not rely too heavily on any one indicator.

Low volatility today does not mean low volatility tomorrow. If volatility jumps from 16% to 32% overnight, and IV moves from predicting a 1% daily move to a 2% daily move, then the statistics of success or failure change accordingly and all those high probabilities you were counting on shrink significantly.

Some traders are contrarian in terms of IV. They see a high IV and think the price will go down or vice versa. Sometimes that works and sometimes it doesn't.

The point is that IV is simply a number. Even though IV is one of the most important, relevant, and useful pieces of information, it has limited value because it can change dramatically from one day to the next. More significantly, IV provides a critical reference point in trading options. IV means that an option with an IV of 20% would be less expensive if it were at 15% and more expensive if it were at 25%. Therefore, as an options seller, you need a good reason to believe that the options are mispriced in your favor.

First you need to understand why IV goes up or down. The answer comes from understanding various reasons why traders buy or sell options. Your strategy is to make money from time decay. Some traders buy options as a leveraged proxy for stocks. Others buy options as a hedge. Perhaps a trader has a large position in a particular stock and wants to buy some puts to ensure profits because he is concerned that the stock might turn downward. He could just sell the stock, of course, but he might not want to for various reasons, short-term capital gains being high among them. He also might not be convinced that the stock will go down permanently.

Another trader could be shorting the stock and could buy calls to hedge that position. People panic more when stock prices fall because they tend to fall a lot faster than they rise. So if markets start taking significant steps down, traders may buy puts to hedge their positions, and the more worried they are, the more they are willing to pay for that protection. This is why volatility is frequently referred to as a "fear" indicator.

Actually it is more of a "hedge" indicator and how much traders are willing to pay for that hedge. Of course, the "fear" priced in could be under- or over-priced. This market psychology explains why trading the math also may mean trading the fear in the market at the moment.

Imagine having the right to buy fire insurance on your house even after the fire started. As the fire starts to spread, the price of that insurance starts to go way up. You'll buy that insurance as long as insurance costs less than the repairs or the house itself. You know you'll pay way more for that insurance even to the point of overpaying.

From a practical trading standpoint, think of IV as a thermometer that measures actual current temperature. When it is high the option prices are high, and when it is low the prices are low. As an options seller, you are not concerned so much with the amount of premium you get on the sale. Granted, it feels great to get a 20% credit on margin rather than 12%, but what does matter is the percentage change in the volatility. A 20% credit doesn't feel so great when the IV moves up 50% over the next few days.

Volatility also doesn't give you an accurate indication of the slope of the price action. If IV stays low, the stock price can keep rising higher and higher. A low IV is an indication of complacency. The level of the complacency can stay relatively stable while the stock keeps going straight up aggressively.

CSI: Condor

Since there are options on almost everything, you could theoretically do condor trades with almost any stock, index, exchange traded fund (ETF), or future. You need to narrow down the playing field as much as possible so your trade has the greatest chance for success. So you need to work backward and profile what a good condor looks like and then find candidates that best fit that model.

First you have to look at which type of underlying stock is practical for condors. Low-priced stocks are no good because there are not enough strike prices on the put side to make a condor work. There could be only two or three strikes on the put side. The goal with condors is to sell far out-of-the-money options. Low-priced stocks may undermine this goal.

Low-priced stocks can also move a great deal suddenly in both percentage and real terms. A good piece of news can move a $5 stock to a $10 overnight. A bad piece of news can take a $10 stock to a $2 stock, and then there is no way to maneuver or shift the condor. So the price of the underlying stock or index has to be high enough that we can adjust the condor, and there have to be enough strikes with enough value to make condors viable.

Even if the gap is not merely at the opening but the stock moves aggressively for several days, the stock could burst right through one of the strike prices. For example, Apple closed at 122 on May 22, 2009. It then proceeded to move straight up for the next nine trading sessions before closing at 145, a 19% move. That was great if you were bullish Apple, but a June condor at 10 Deltas (more about this later) would have had a range from 105 to 140. A sudden move to 145 would definitely have ruined your day.

Liquidity requires having plenty of traders on the other side of the trade. This is especially important in a fast-moving market. You might try to buy to close your condor or adjust one of the wings and find that no one is interested. The more liquid the market, the less this becomes an issue; for most of the large cap, publicly traded companies, options trading has plenty of liquidity. This problem is more likely to be seen in low-volume OTC stocks. Liquidity also affects the bid-ask spread. You want to trade condors on underlying stocks that experience a large volume of shares traded each day, and high open interest, so pricing stays reasonable without huge spreads between the bid and the ask.

Price of the underlying stock, a healthy number of strikes, and liquidity are key elements in picking the condor. You also want some fundamental reason for picking a stock. A stock whose price cannot be easily manipulated by large investors is very desirable. It wouldn't prevent large moves but it could minimize their impact on price. One indication that a stock cannot be easily manipulated is market cap (total dollar value of all outstanding stock). A company worth billions of dollars is going to be harder to push up or down more than a few dollars by any large institution because there will always be buyers and sellers to take advantage of price action. Large market cap isn't enough by itself to make a stock a good candidate, however.

For example, as shown in Figure 1.9, ConAgra (CAG) reported market cap of $9.6 billion in August 2010. Over time, the price has stayed roughly in a sideways range. For months at a time, it frequently stayed within a $2 to $7 trading range. (By August 2010, the 1-year range was approximately $19 to $26.)

Source: thinkorswim by TD Ameritrade

FIGURE 1.9   *ConAgra graph*

At this point, it looked like a good stock for trading condors. However, from the options profile it didn't look as attractive.

The price in Figure 1.10 was $25, right at the $25 strike. There were only two strikes above 25 on the call side, and neither had any value to speak of even 5 months out. The put side was not much better, although a small bump in value appeared at the September 20 puts. Open interest (the number of outstanding contracts) was tiny for such a big company, and the volume was nonexistent. Even if you could trade a condor, it would be difficult to get out quickly or make an adjustment in a fast market.

The fact that a stock is a poor candidate for condors is because the options prices are conveying important information about the future of the price.

Actuals	CAG Common		Legend	
	25.00	-0.23	MktPr	Chg

Options	APR <5>		MAY <40>		JUN <68>		SEP <159>		
	O.I.	Volume	O.I.	Volume	O.I.	Volume	O.I.	Volume	
45.0 calls									
40.0 calls									
35.0 calls									
30.0 calls	101		50		444		1250		
25.0 calls>	1990	3	828	58	7980	4	4220		
22.5 calls	665		14		2470		642		
20.0 calls	2		29		1750		1		
17.5 calls									
40.0 puts									
35.0 puts			4						
30.0 puts	4		20		98		6		
25.0 puts>	1920		847	1	1580		1770		
22.5 puts	50		98	77	2340		5270	3	
20.0 puts					925		1160		
17.5 puts					2220				
15.0 puts					39				

Source: OptionVue 6

FIGURE 1.10   *Open interest (O.I) and volume for ConAgra*

A great deal of current information is available about market opinion within the options prices that is not available with stocks. With stocks you merely see a price and efficient market theory says all available information is reflected within the price with no indication of future activity. With options you see a much richer picture. For every month, the 30 calls were selling for 0.05. With this information do you think it was a good time to buy stock in ConAgra? This doesn't mean that the stock couldn't go up, but options sellers were putting themselves at considerable risk for a mere five cents if they were wrong. The 20 puts didn't fare much better.

Google (GOOG) provides a vastly different example. As shown in Figure 1.11, the stock was priced at $572. In August 2010, the company had market cap of $121.2 billion. This is not an easy stock to manipulate.

Actuals	GOOG Common		Legend	
	572.73	+6.51	MktPr	Chg

Options	APR <5>		MAY <40>		JUN <68>		SEP <159>	
600 calls	O.I.	Volume	O.I.	Volume	O.I.	Volume	O.I.	Volume
590 calls	8180	2190	1600	289	1550	175	1610	45
580 calls	7700	2880	988	928	1990	643	177	71
570 calls>	8020	3030	1550	1040	2630	324	1270	146
560 calls	5280	1200	1140	359	1370	177	235	18
550 calls	4450	703	936	113	2380	49	391	20
540 calls	3190	465	312	58	1310	9	495	12
530 calls	2880	189	127	53	552	14	250	
520 calls	693	57	309	45	406	6	121	1
580 puts	2060	514	477	114	745	5	167	
570 puts>	3180	2170	585	669	1890	101	181	1
560 puts	4240	1220	734	368	1190	433	407	39
550 puts	6460	1970	810	487	1690	111	550	5
540 puts	5860	1990	1010	395	1170	613	249	20
530 puts	9300	2510	1920	182	1210	127	347	6
520 puts	9900	1880	1890	173	935	118	1440	2
510 puts	7650	1130	4140	157	1920	436	160	36

Source: OptionVue 6

FIGURE 1.11   *Open interest and volume for Google*

Liquidity was not a problem because open interest and volume were very high for Google, true in any month and at any price. Strikes traded at $10 intervals. Because Google was priced at a high of $572 in this chart's period, the number of strikes to trade condors was more than sufficient. Although not visible here, the range of strikes available ranged from 350 to 740 for May and to 930 for June.

Even so, the history of Google's chart in Figure 1.12 reveals some obvious red flags for trading condors. The price swings for Google have ranged from $747 down to $250 and back up to $644, a 66% move down and a 144% move up—not exactly a sideways-moving stock.

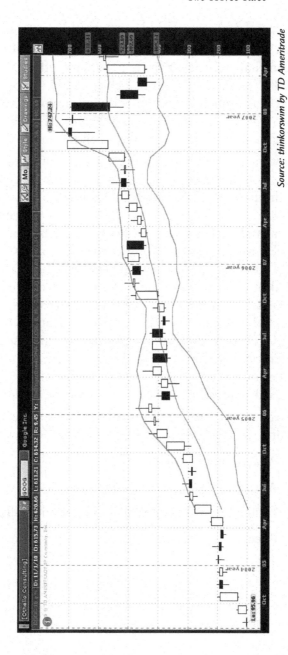

FIGURE 1.12   *Google trending graph*

Source: thinkorswim by TD Ameritrade

Google's chart shows that even when a company has high market cap and isn't easily manipulated, it doesn't mean that news can't have a dramatic effect. In April 2008, Google jumped from a close at 450 up to 535 the next day, following their earnings announcement, a 19% opening gap as depicted in Figure 1.13. This is not the condition you want to see when trading condors.

So, are any stocks appropriate for condors? When news comes out regarding a company, the reaction can be dramatic and sudden. Earnings reports may cause a stock to surge or fall apart quickly. Decisions from governmental agencies like the FDA affect pharmaceutical stocks. Regulatory decisions by the EPA or FCC, or the need to obtain government contracts, all can make or break a company overnight. Sometimes the timing of those decisions is known in advance and sometimes it is not. Other events like a criminal investigation, firing of the CEO, or a hostile takeover are all unplanned and unanticipated events. As in the horse-race example, the jockey on the lead horse could suddenly fall off; then all the odds and values would change for the other horses.

To review the profile of a company desirable for trading condors, it should possess all the following:

- A large number of strikes
- A reasonably high-priced underlying stock
- High liquidity in both open interest and volume
- Price not dramatically affected by specific news

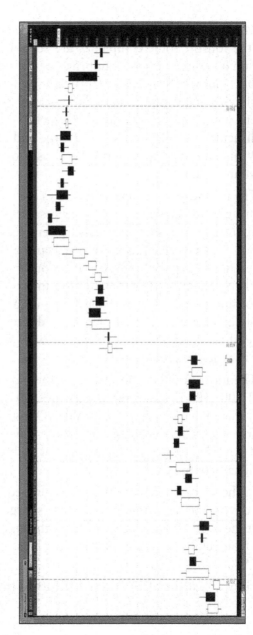

Source: thinkorswim by TD Ameritrade

FIGURE 1.13 *Google earnings gap*

Many companies have the first three elements but not the fourth. Some companies are so well diversified that no one piece of news can brutalize the stock. These include Johnson & Johnson (JNJ). But they suffer from not having a lot of far out-of-the-money strikes with decent value and too few available strikes; so it would be difficult to trade condors on a large and stable company like JNJ due to too-low IV, thus too-low option premium values.

The best way to overcome the news effect is to dilute it through an index. An index represents a basket of companies. Sometimes they can be very sector specific like oil or pharmaceuticals, or they can be very broad, representing the whole stock market or large swaths of it. The problem with sector-specific indexes is that an important piece of news regarding oil can affect the whole oil sector and move the index dramatically. The more diversified the index, the greater the dilution effect, which blunts the effect of the news.

The most popular and traded of the indexes are the S&P 500 (SPX), which represents the 500 largest publicly traded companies; the NASDAQ (NDX), which mostly represents the technology sector; and the Russell 2000 (RUT), which represents 2,000 publicly traded small cap companies.

In the Google example the stock jumped 19% from one day to the next. In contrast to this large move, the most the S&P 500 moved from 1990 through 2010 was up (from close to close) 11%. The most it dropped was 9%.

How about the other three elements of the profile?

You want high-priced options allowing you to create large condors, and you want a large number of option strikes to give you flexibility. In considering the three indexes, they all have had historically high prices. The SPX has the most strike intervals. The actual intervals are less important than the fact that all the intervals are heavily traded.

Look at the open interest on these three indexes. Table 1.1 is a snapshot taken on April 13, 2010, of about 5 months' worth of options. The average, median (so as to take out the effect of extreme highs and lows), and highest open interest (to show just how large the market can be) are presented in Table 1.2. For liquidity, nothing beats the SPX.

TABLE 1.1

	Range Low	Range High	Strike Intervals
SPX	666	1,576	5
RUT	324	856	10
NDX	795	4,147	25

Source: OptionVue 6

TABLE 1.2

	Avg OI	Median OI	High
SPX	42,839	27,551	191,487
RUT	3,909	1,598	21,798
NDX	1,749	629	14,011

Source: OptionVue 6

The profile identifies the best candidates for trading condors. There are other reasons these are good trading candidates. You could call these "bonus features."

American- and European-Style Options

The most frequently asked question asked about condors is the famous "what if" question: What if the market goes through the wings of the condor because of a crash of some sort? Although serious loss is always a real possibility, there are ways to help mitigate this risk. One way is through the diluted effect any one company or even sectorwide news has on diversified indexes. You can adjust condors and use exit strategies. Another safeguard comes from the *type* of option you trade.

One danger that option traders are exposed to is assignment. For example, if you sold a 100 put and the price dropped right through that strike price to $80, the person who bought that put from you could exercise his option right away and lock in his profit. This means he can buy 100 shares at current market value of $80 and sell them to you for $100 by exercising the put. The buyer of the put does *not* have to wait until expiration to exercise this right. The vast majority of options are American-style options, meaning they can be exercised at any time.

The SPY is an ETF that trades on the exchange just like a stock and that closely mimics the S&P 500 index. Its prices are one-tenth of the full S&P. What is nice about this ETF is that it is very liquid, it's electronically traded, and the difference between the bid and the ask is almost nonexistent. However, the SPY trades using American-style options. If you sell a condor in the SPY and the market goes right through one of the wings, you risk having the options exercised immediately. On the face of it, this might seem unfair. After all, you entered this trade thinking there were probabilities in your favor that the market would expire within your condor, and now you are forced to take the loss. Unfortunately, that is one of the risks of trading American-style options.

There is another type of option called European style. Unlike American-style options that can be exercised at any time, *these options cannot be exercised until the actual day of expiration.* Why is this beneficial? If you sell a 100 put and the price drops to $80, you still have a month until expiration. This is potentially a huge safety net. Losses can't be forced upon you until the last trading day. If you do take a loss, it is because you decided to buy to close the options at a loss. However, if you hold on and the stock rallies back over $100 by expiration day, you will have lost nothing.

Most indexes trade using European-style options, including the SPX, RUT, and NDX. Nobody wants to experience the scenario where the price breaks through one of the wings and one side of the condor is assigned. European-style options take a shade more risk off the table because occasionally time does heal market wounds.

Hedging Effect

Why would buyers overpay for options? So far buyers look like speculators. They have a directional bias and buy a call, a put, or some combination thereof. Others use options primarily as a hedge to prevent significant losses.

Why not just use a stop loss that executes at a predetermined price and not incur the costs of buying a put? One reason is that a stock could gap down far below the stop loss and may execute at whatever the market price is for that stock. So instead of incurring a 10% loss, you could suddenly find yourself with a 20% loss.

The other reason not to put in a stop loss is to prevent a taxable event. If the stock you bought has doubled in value since you bought it 3 months ago, a stop loss to protect the profit triggers a short-term capital gains tax. In that situation buying a put, though costly, is less expensive than the tax consequences of the stop loss kicking in. The put offsets the loss with increased premium value, but without requiring you to dispose of shares.

What if you had a portfolio of 50 stocks and you wanted to hedge the portfolio from a drop in the market? You could buy puts on each individual stock. The fees involved for each transaction would be prohibitive. And you may not own a round number of 100 lot stocks for each company, complicating the insurance put even more.

Many investors watch each individual stock move up and down in value each day. They know that they have a "portfolio" but act as though they own a bunch of unrelated stocks. Their portfolio might be down but it's because stock xyz is down a lot and has offset small gains elsewhere.

The sophisticated investor knows the Beta of his portfolio. Beta is the relationship of the stock or portfolio to the overall market or S&P 500. A Beta of 1 means if the market moves up or down 1%, then the stock should correspondingly move up or down 1%. Apple had a Beta of 1.5 at the chart date, so it should move +(-)1.5% as the market moves +(-)1%. ConAgra had a Beta of 0.8 so its moves should be less volatile than the overall market, at about 80%. So if you hold many stocks in your portfolio, the entire holding has its own net collective Beta.

You could hedge your entire portfolio based on its Beta by buying the right number of puts on the S&P 500. You would be wise to always know the Beta of your portfolio with this hedging solution in mind. It explains why your portfolio may be outperforming or underperforming the market.

The Volatility Gap

Even though hedging provides a good reason for over-valued options, you would still like to see some evidence that options are overvalued. There is another kind of volatility, historic or statistical volatility (SV). Implied volatility is the market prediction of future movement derived from the option's price, and statistical volatility is a measure of past movement. Comparing these two types of volatility, what was predicted versus what actually happened, is useful for deciding what underlying stocks to trade.

It is reasonable at this stage to confirm that in fact IV is historically higher than SV. After establishing that this is the norm, you can move forward and feel comfortable selling options on the underlying stock. The past is no prologue for the future, but what you're looking for is a probability in your favor so that you are confident enough to commit to trading in the index.

There are several software tools that can help identify candidates with a skew between IV and SV. Since you have ruled out stocks, you are interested only in which indexes are the most likely to report the necessary skew. The report shown in Figure 1.14 looks at the past 800 trading days and divides the average SV by the Average IV. Anything over 1 in the "Sort Value" column has a favorable volatility skew. The report confirms that the three indexes have a historical edge in favor of the seller since the average IV tends to be higher than the volatility realized.

OPSCAN Report   04/21/10 @ 21:41
DO Chronically Overvalued Options (Indexes)

Picked by ATVOL$(10)>10, IV(100)>1
Sorted by AIV(800)/ASV(800)
Showing AIV(800), ASV(800), ATVOL$(10), LASTU, IV, SV, LIV(800), HIV(800)
Including Indexes

The information contained in this report is for the private use of
the subscriber only. Make no investments based solely on
this report, without careful research.

		Sort			Avg.Tot	Underly				
Asset Name	Symbol	Value	Avg.IV (800)	Avg.SV (800)	$Volume (10)	Last	IV	SV	Low.IV (800)	High.IV (800)
1. Yen Index (PHX)	XDN	1.24	14.8	11.9	36	107.36	10.2	8.6	9.4	32.3
2. Euro Index (PHX)	XDE	1.20	12.2	10.2	64	133.87	10.0	8.6	4.7	26.8
3. Brit Pound Inx (PHX)	XDB	1.16	12.5	10.8	24	154.06	11.8	8.1	3.1	27.6
4. Euro Index (ISE)	EUI	1.13	12.4	11.0	11	74.68	10.0	8.4	5.9	27.6
5. Can Dollar Inx (PHX)	XDC	1.08	14.5	13.4	24	100.01	9.8	8.3	8.2	27.1
6. S&P SmallCap 600 Index	SML	1.05	30.8	29.2	18	366.09	22.4	15.4	14.8	69.7
7. Russell 2000 Index	RUT	1.04	31.1	29.9	75026	726.19	19.0	16.2	15.1	75.2
8. S&P 100 Index	OEX	1.04	24.4	23.5	9014	550.05	13.8	10.7	10.1	71.3
9. Austr Dollar Inx (PHX)	XDA	1.04	18.2	17.5	17	92.60	10.4	8.6	9.0	42.1
10. Nasdaq 100 Index	NDX	1.03	27.2	26.3	72064	2034.75	15.2	12.7	14.8	69.2
11. S&P 500 Index (future)	SP	1.03	25.1	24.4	49387	1196.78	14.7	11.8	9.7	72.6
12. Mini SPX Index (CBOE)	XSP	1.02	25.2	24.6	84	120.59	14.5	11.3	10.8	67.0
13. S&P 500 Index	SPX	1.02	25.0	24.4	697340	1205.94	14.2	11.1	10.4	67.4
14. Morgan Stanley Retail	MVR	1.02	37.3	36.6	14	208.08	20.2	17.1	16.8	92.3
15. Dow Jones Index	DJX	1.02	23.2	22.8	1639	111.25	12.8	10.3	10.1	65.9
16. S&P 100 Index	XEO	1.00	23.8	23.8	3805	550.05	13.3	11.0	9.8	70.0
17. Volatility Index (SPX)	VIX	1.00	109.7	109.7	44923	16.32	187.3	76.7	56.7	297.2
18. S&P Midcap Index	MID	1.00	28.2	28.2	156	831.76	16.2	14.9	12.6	73.2
19. Semiconductor Index	SOX	0.97	34.4	35.6	1043	391.46	27.0	24.9	19.5	74.9
20. Mini-Dow (future)	YM	0.95	23.2	24.3	582	110.36	11.7	10.6	10.3	66.6
21. Housing Index (PHLX)	HGX	0.93	46.0	49.4	12	123.13	28.1	23.6	23.2	89.2
22. Gold/Silver Index	XAU	0.93	45.7	49.3	832	168.62	30.6	26.6	26.7	100.2
23. E-Mini Nas-100 (future	NQ	0.92	27.3	29.7	1183	2020.07	15.4	13.4	14.3	68.0
24. Cyclical Index (MS)	CYC	0.92	32.6	35.5	38	950.33	22.3	18.3	11.8	69.2
25. Oil Service Index (PHL	OSX	0.90	42.2	46.8	790	217.97	26.6	25.5	24.4	100.2
26. Natural Gas Index	XNG	0.90	35.5	39.6	123	561.57	21.8	19.7	17.5	86.3
27. Mini-Nasdaq 100 Index	MNX	0.87	26.6	30.6	1096	203.45	15.1	12.7	14.5	67.9
28. E-Mini S&P 500 (future	ES	0.85	24.9	29.2	28822	1197.15	14.4	12.1	9.9	69.4

Source: OptionVue 6

FIGURE 1.14   *OPSCAN report*

Why not trade the Yen Index since it is the one with the best skew? The volume on the Yen and almost all the other indexes disqualifies them as good candidates for condors.[2] Liquidity should never be overlooked whether you are trading condors on indexes or on stocks.

Of course, 800 days is a long time. How do the different indexes fare in different timeframes? In Table 1.3, you will find consistency in the volatility skew in favor of the seller over multiple timeframes (as of 4/21/2010).

The skew does not tell the whole story. Figure 1.15 is a graphical representation of volatility for the SPX. The lower line represents SV and the upper line represents IV. There is a consistent gap between the two types. It looks as though a seller of volatility would have the edge, and if so it is money in the bank. Looks, however, can be deceiving.

Source: OptionVue 6

FIGURE 1.15   *Graph of volatility gap tells only part of the story*

If you view your trade simply as a volatility trade, the edge would exist. However, you are selling condors and not just volatility. Time is also involved and it changes everything. You don't want to over-rely on the probabilities, and you need to manage your actual risk very carefully.

---

2. *The only exception is the S&P 500 futures. Trading option condors on the S&P futures is doable but is complicated by ever-changing margin requirements, adding a layer of complication you don't need.*

TABLE 1.3

SPX

Averages	3 weeks	6 weeks	10 weeks	1.5 years	3 years	4.5 years	6 years
Statistical	10.8%	11.1%	13.5%	29.3%	25.0%	20.2%	19.1%
Implied	14.2%	14.7%	15.8%	29.4%	25.5%	20.8%	19.7%

Source: OptionVue 6

RUT

Averages	3 weeks	6 weeks	10 weeks	1.5 years	3 years	4.5 years	6 years
Statistical	15.4%	15.3%	17.1%	35.1%	30.4%	26.0%	24.9%
Implied	19.5%	19.6%	20.3%	36.1%	31.5%	27.3%	26.2%

Source: OptionVue 6

NDX

Averages	3 weeks	6 weeks	10 weeks	1.5 years	3 years	4.5 years	6 years
Statistical	12.3%	12.7%	15.2%	29.3%	26.6%	23.4%	22.3%
Implied	15.4%	15.9%	16.9%	30.3%	27.6%	27.1%	25.6%

Source: OptionVue 6

Not solely depending on a volatility skew is important because many condor sellers have lost money in this time interval. How could that be if a persistent skew like this exists? A market with falling IV is a sign of complacency, not direction. This complacency doesn't only mean that the market is moving sideways. It may also mean that it is rising. Any gain through diminishing volatility (Vega) can be overcome through the rapid rise (Gamma) in price, as shown in Figure 1.16.

Condors were actually a challenge to maneuver in this environment, and those who did not tread carefully lost a lot of money. In particular, the market jumps in July 2009 and the market rally from February to April 2010 were frightening for most traders relying on market-neutral strategies. How to maneuver these kinds of markets is both interesting and revealing, and is explained in the next chapter.

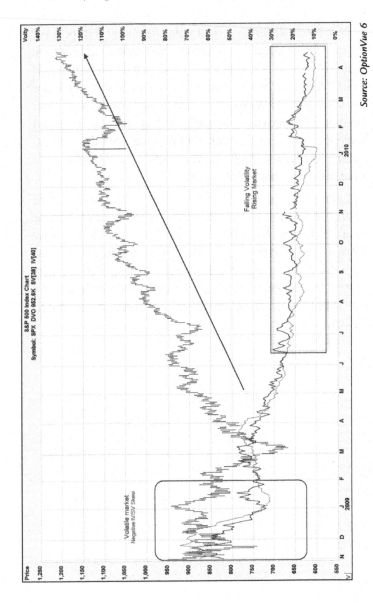

FIGURE 1.16   *The correlation (or lack of it) between volatility and price action*

Source: OptionVue 6

Chapter 2

Placing a Trade

Indexes are probably the best instruments to trade condors, and the SPX, RUT, and NDX are the best of this group. The two main reasons are liquidity and their use of European-style options. The greater the liquidity, the easier it is to execute the trade, and European-style options increase your safety by eliminating the risk of early exercise.

The buying and selling of contracts takes place through an auction process. The bid represents what the buyer wants to pay, and the ask is the price the seller is seeking. There is no right way or wrong way to approach the bid-ask spread, but how you negotiate the price will result in different outcomes in your trading.

In an electronic market the difference between the two can be negligible. Whereas the rest of the trading world has gone electronic, the indexes are traded the old-fashioned way, by open outcry. As in the old movies of the stock exchange, traders are yelling back and forth, frantically buying and selling with hand signals. One day these will also go the way of complete electronic trading, but until then the bid-ask spread you see on your screen will unfortunately not always be the price you can get. There is frequently a large discrepancy in the bid-ask on the computer screen and what is actually traded in the pit. The computer can show a spread that is dollars apart when the pit may be dimes apart. Therefore, the midpoint between the bid and ask is a good generalized reference for analyzing how trades work out. The midpoint, where the market is most likely to trade, is a pretty accurate and usable price.

There is no absolutely right or wrong way to decide which strikes to use, but remember, not all trades are equal. Going through the different strategies, you will decide how to approach the market.

Two Out of Three

Getting into a trade and getting out of a trade is what condors are all about. Everything that happens in between is just noise. Each trader has his own style. Your goal may be to trade as conservatively as possible. But trading condors is risky business. Even within a risky strategy, there are different degrees of risk taking.

The inevitable forward motion of time is a two-edged sword. On the one hand, the longer you stay in a condor, the greater your potential return. On the other hand, every day you are in the market is another day exposed to market risk. Everybody loves reward, but risk is frightful. An overly aggressive approach to trading just isn't worth the sleepless nights.

There are numerous ways to trade condors. Be aware of all the important considerations before you make the trade. Condors are very slow-moving creatures. When you sell a condor, time decay occurs slowly at first. Don't make any decision too hastily. Moving in and out of a trade too quickly is expensive simply from the bid-ask spread. If the bid-ask spread for a condor is $3.50–$4.00, then it sells, without negotiating, for $3.50 but is purchased for $4.00. So if you sold a condor and flipped it immediately, you would be out 0.50 a share. This can be a big loss for simply getting in and out of a trade. Patience really is a virtue when trading condors. You have to be patient each step of the way, whether you are getting into a trade or adjusting a trade. The only time you should be impatient is when taking a profit.

Many condor traders are in the market every single day of the year. This may not be the best approach but it is a legitimate strategy for some. You can make or lose money only if you are in the market. The strategy of staying in the market as little as possible and maximizing profits as much as possible is the most desirable.

Successful trading is all about having a plan. Without a plan you become victim to the two killers of all trading, greed and fear. Let the plan make the decisions instead of greed or fear making them. Trading plans may be prepared in advance not as a decision model but as a reaction model, which lets you take advantage of greed and fear in other traders. All aspects of the trade, entry, adjustment, and exit, are conscious tactical and strategic *reactions* to the market.

Trading works best when it is set up as a *reaction* to the market. As much as you want to, you will never be able to move the market one way or the other through sheer force of will or prediction. Confidence or worry will not have any effect on either the market or your success. If you keep this simple fact in mind, your experience will be a lot less stressful. Proper planning is simply making decisions in advance so that you can react appropriately when the time comes.

The only time in the trading process when you do not simply react to market conditions is when you enter the trade. Therefore you need to define your conditions for waiting for the right moment, entering a trade, and committing yourself. Because you choose the when and where of your point of entry, you have the leisure to make sure your trade fulfills all your predetermined conditions so that you don't have to compromise on your goals.

When entering a condor, you hope that the market will stay range bound (1) within your wings long enough (2) to make the profit (3) you seek. Knowing what you want, "range bound," "long enough," and "profit," defines the trade. There are three considerations when selling condors:

1. Time

2. Position

3. Price

A perfect condor strategy is one in which the trader knows exactly how many days away from expiration he should put in his trade, exactly which strikes to sell in his vertical spreads, and the correct amount of credit he wants for the trade. Of course, this never happens because you can never purposely get every decision right in advance. To make a profit with condors, think of condor trading as the "Art of the Imperfect Trade." You don't have to be exactly right, just approximately right.

Unfortunately, these three conditions are frequently intertwined and it is difficult to consider one without the other two. Since volatility is the wildcard in options trading, you will not know whether your trade met all three conditions perfectly until after you are out of the trade. Staring at the choices in front of you prior to making a trade, you will frequently find that the best you can do is to compromise and choose two out of three of these considerations for your condor. The question is which two out of three?

Time

The heart and soul of a condor trade is time decay or Theta. The immediate enemy of Theta is volatility or Vega. If you choose to sell a condor with an expiration date 6 months out, a lot of things can happen. If the price does nothing, time decay will progress at a nice clip, but if there are sudden price movements, especially on the downside, the position could start losing value very quickly.

What does it mean when a condor is losing value? You sell condors for one price. If the value of the condor goes up because of volatility, it can become more expensive to "buy" back the condor you sold. In that case you would have sold high and bought higher. Although not always avoidable, this is a scenario you want avoid as much as possible.

There is an important give and take between Theta and Vega. You don't want to go so far out in time that the initial time decay is too small for the risk involved. A jump in volatility or Vega would devour any time decay you accumulated and then some. All of a sudden you could find yourself with a condor already in the red with such a small Theta that you are barely whittling away at the loss caused by the increase in Vega. On the other hand, you don't want to sell a condor too close to expiration because value could be too low to get a decent premium; then you run the risk of the price falling outside of your price ranges.

Table 2.1 gives a snapshot of three different condors and expirations. The only thing they have in common is that the Deltas of the options sold are approximately 10.

TABLE 2.1   *Comparing Condors with Equivalent Deltas and Credits with Different Times to Expiration**

Puts 1100/1105, Calls 1220/1225, Credit $105, Expiration 17 Days	
Theta	4.48
Vega	−11.90
Puts 1055/1060, Calls, 1255/1260, Credit $99, Expiration 45 Days	
Theta	3.52
Vega	−11.72
Puts 1025/1030, Calls 1275/1280, Credit $130, Expiration 73 Days	
Theta	1.39
Vega	−11.81

*May 4, 2010, VIX 25, S&P 1168, Margin requirement $500.
Source: OptionVue 6

In all three examples, the Vega told you that with every 1% increase in implied volatility, the condor would gain $11 in value. Since you want the condor to lose value, anything that makes it gain works against you. On the other hand, Theta told you how much value the condor would lose per day just from the passage of time. Your goal may be to keep only one-third of the initial credit and then buy to close the condor. Use this "keep one third as profit" as your objective to evaluate the three approaches.

Start with the furthest example, of 73 days. With a Theta of 1.4, it would take about 30 days for the condor to deteriorate $43, or one-third of the initial credit. Keep in mind that Theta is not constant but normally increases quickly over time. Theta is kept constant in this example to keep things simple and to highlight the relationship between Theta and Vega. With 73 days remaining, you have about an 11-to-1 ratio. A 1% increase in volatility would eat up 11 days of time decay. What you lose in Theta, however, you gain in the size of the condor, which is 245 points from side to side.

The second condor with 45 days has a different ratio profile of 11 to 3 with a spread of 195 points from end to end. For the third condor, with only 17 days remaining, the Vega-to-Theta ratio is 11 to 4 but the condor is only 115 points wide. The closer you are to expiration, the narrower the ratio of Vega to Theta becomes, which is positive, but it comes at the expense of the condor's size.

At what point does the Vega-to-Theta ratio become too large? Your goal is to capture relatively small profits and give up the rest, hopefully in a 2- to 4-week period. Sometimes this is just as possible with a longer-term option trade as a shorter-term trade. If Theta or Vega were your only concerns, you could just sell condors as close as possible to expiration. Although this strategy is doable, it is not recommended.

The flip side of a problem can present an important and significant opportunity. Emphasis has been on the effect of volatility rising on your condor. What happens if there is a 1% *decrease* in volatility? On the 73-day trade, a 1% drop would give you an 11-day head start on your condor. A drop in volatility translates to a quick profit. This is not an unlikely occurrence. The advantage of not being in the market every day of the year is that you get to wait and pick your entry points. If you spot an unusual spike in volatility on a particular day, it might be a great time to sell a condor. When volatility goes up, prices also go up. If the market settles down after it digests the news that caused the spike in volatility, then volatility will also settle down. Lower volatility leads to lower option prices. In this scenario, you could potentially sell a condor on a volatility spike and even buy to close the same day and make a nice profit. On the other hand, just because volatility jumps, it doesn't necessarily mean that volatility will go back down immediately. Very frequently a jump in volatility is also a precursor to a few more large moves in volatility. Either way, it's a chance you take. Usually, the odds are in your favor if the market panics and overreacts.

So how far out in time should you go to place the trade? There are a lot of potential trading rules for how many days away from expiration you should pick. Many of these ideas work most of the time. For example, many traders jump back in the market the day after expiration. The overabundance of buyers can have a dampening effect on the prices, so it might not always be a good time to enter the market immediately after expiration. Unfortunately, the most favored trade is about a month from expiration. From the Vega/Theta perspective this seems to be the most favorable. However, when things go wrong and market prices start flying all over the place, adjustments to an open condor can get pretty scary and expensive. You might find yourself at the whim of the market during expiration week feeling like a day trader praying for the right opportunity to get out.

Other timeframes work better from a risk-management standpoint. For instance, a condor could be placed the Friday before the previous month's expiration, so, depending on the length of the period between expirations, that could be anywhere from 5 to 6 weeks out in time. Getting in between 7 and 8 weeks from expiration also may be advantageous based on the balance between time value and time. You can't always use an inflexible rule for timing because there are too many other considerations, such as volatility, price, and position.

Going out more than 70 days brings in a great deal of Vega risk relative to Theta. What reason would there be to trade that far out? One scenario is when volatility is very, very low during a sustained market rally. Since sharp rallies are suspect because of the adage and experience that markets don't "fall up," you might believe that the rally looks too vulnerable and you then fear that the market could correct sharply. You could wait for that correction to happen but you might end up waiting a long time. In the market rally of 2009–2010, price knew only how to go one way: up. Many condor traders with their rules to trade just a few weeks away from expiration had condors that were too small, and they ended up losing a lot of money as the market "fell up." If the market is trending, make sure that your condor has room to accommodate both the trend and a sudden reversal. If the condor is too small for your tastes 6 weeks out, consider the next month's options, which might take you out 10 weeks instead.

How about when the volatility is very high as in a falling market? If you catch the end of the downtrend, you might get the best of both worlds, selling high volatility in a consolidating market. Then you get the benefits of falling volatility and time decay. The other danger is when the market rebounds up too quickly. This is called Gamma risk and that can overcome both Theta and Vega.

It is misguided to assume that there is a best number of days before expiration to place a trade. The best recommendation is to stay away from any trade less than 5 weeks away from expiration and preferably enter longer-term trades. Not trading until the right opportunity comes along is a key part of the trading strategy.

Position

The element of time is a primary concern to clarify the "when" of putting on a condor trade. Now you need to decide the "where" of placing the wings of your condor, which is going to take a bit of educated guesswork about future market behavior. Fortunately, that guesswork can be off the mark and still end up profitable. There are three methods for predicting future market behavior: fundamental analysis, technical analysis, and volatility analysis.

Before prognosticating, make a real effort to convince yourself that any idea or claim that suggests an edge in direction derived from analysis is wrong. There are just too many variables. Use charts and the news to get a sense of market direction and the strength of that direction, however, also trade based on assuming the worst in either direction. Not having an opinion about market direction is harder than you think. It means assuming that all the websites and news outlets could be wrong.

Behavioral finance teaches that the average person thinks he is smarter than the average person. The ordinary investor also tends to attribute his profitable trades to intelligence and hard work. Losses, on the other hand, are attributed to bad luck. The sad truth is probably just the opposite. Success for most is more likely a matter of luck, whereas failure is the result of poor judgment. Remember, even smart people get it wrong regularly. This is why condor traders try to move the odds in their favor as much as possible without basing their trades on their own abilities. That way, even when they are wrong they can make a profit.

Fundamentals

The traditional way to form an opinion about the market is to use fundamental analysis. Using a variety of analytical methods to understand the underpinnings of the economy, politics, weather, and everything that makes the world go around, economists try to predict future market behavior. Fundamental analysis is of limited use to condor traders because condors require short-term trading and fundamentals are better applied to long-term investing. You don't really care about the long-term health of the economy as far as your trade is concerned. You're interested only in the stability of the stock's price over the next 2 to 4 weeks. Stability does not mean merely staying in a narrow range. "Stability" means price is stable enough to stay in the profit range of your condor. So if your condor is 300 points wide, the stability we're ultimately looking for is limited to 300 points. Fundamental analysts are usually longer term in their projections, which really doesn't help you at all. Typically, only truly unexpected news rocks markets. You know you are a victim of fundamental analysis if you are watching CNBC all day or if you have subscribed to several newsletters all with the goal of trying to understand "why" the market moved a certain way and "why" it is going to move a certain way in the future. Even floor traders frequently don't know why the market is moving one way or another on any given day. Just because an "expert" conveys his opinion with absolute confidence does not make him correct.

As mentioned earlier, try not to have too strong an opinion about which way the market is going to go. This is not to say that you should be oblivious to the news. You should have a general sense of the financial mood so you can prepare for the worst. With fundamental analysis you are looking for anything that smells of systemic risk. The kinds of news events that have a pervasive effect on the economy and that have no easy fix, such as bank failures and wars, are the kinds of things you can't ignore and what are termed "systemic." A bad unemployment number or GDP can have a strong effect on the market but the market will recover. With systemic risk, you never know when the problem will be solved, how the "fix" will be received by the market, or just how big the problem may become. Government intervention was the catalyst for pivoting the market straight up after the slide in March 2009. This was completely unpredictable. The subsequent market rally was suspect for months. Hedge funds were not making any money because they were shorting the market all the way up and then covering their shorts.

Reading the *Wall Street Journal, Barron's,* or *BusinessWeek* may just get in the way of your decision-making process. Remember, you are trading the mathematics of options and that takes precedence over opinion. One guaranteed way to lose all your money in the market is to follow the opinions in the news. Bears and bulls are always right, eventually, like a broken clock. But you are an options trader and for you timing is everything. Even if the Bear or the Bull is correct, what really matters is *when* he is correct. Having an opinion *might* work well for a buy-and-hold investor, but being right at the wrong time is the kiss of death for an options trader.

Charts

The next and most popular way, since it *seems* the easiest, is to look at charts. Everybody looks at charts. The dilemma, of course, is deciding whether the charts are conveying any meaningful information. The lure of chart or technical analysis lies in a fundamental problem, the human brain. Perhaps the greatest strength and simultaneous weakness of the human brain is its hard-wired tendency for pattern recognition. We spot patterns even where none exist. Thus the expression "the trend is your friend" can be a deadly trap. However, there is another school of technical analysis that is contrarian, believing every trend ends in a reversal, which is eventually correct, and that by the time you see the trend, the trend is over. How could they both be right? Finally, if any of these ideas really worked, wouldn't everybody do them? We would all turn on our computers and program them to do the exact same trade according to the same set of rules. Of course, then nothing would ever happen because we would all be buyers or sellers at the same time.

Not all technical indicators are created equal. There are some indicators that reveal what *should* happen and others that reveal what *is* happening in an informative way. The better volatility-based indicators reveal the statistical significance of a particular price move relative to previous price moves. Jeff Augen in *Volatility Edge* developed a great indicator that looks at the standard deviation of the change of the price.[1] Because options are all about volatility, it makes sense to use some type of volatility indicators.

---

1. *(C-C[1])/((StandardDev(Log(C[1]/C[2]), 20, 2))*C[1]) where C=Close*

One of the most popular statistical indicators is Bollinger Bands. The bands illustrate a 2 standard deviation move up or down, based on a 20-day moving average of price. Price has a 95% statistical chance of remaining within the range. Bollinger Bands can be useful in a sideways market when the bands are above and below the price range. But when the price trends sharply up or down, the bands can be to the left and right of the price, which is not helpful when you're trying to identify a range. Prices that break out of the bands tend to find their way back. This is not true every time because Bollinger Bands are a lagging indicator, and if there is a dramatic shift in market sentiment price can travel a long time along the upper or lower band.

A volatility chart, which is different from a price chart, can be created for every stock or index. Options software or some online sites will do this for you. Bollinger Bands can be created around these volatility charts. Since the volatility of a stock is assumed to be relatively steady over time, any big changes in volatility are also assumed to be temporary and will eventually revert to the norm. So big volatility spikes through the Bollinger Bands can be viewed as temporary aberrations and will revert to the mean. Pure volatility traders seek these spikes to sell options and buy to close when volatility drops.

One popular measure of the volatility of the S&P 500 is the VIX. When it comes to implied volatility, traders usually refer to the volatility of a specific strike price at-the-money, in-the-money, or out-of-the-money. At-the-money call option volatility is the usual reference point when referring to a stock's or index's implied volatility. The VIX was designed by the CBOE as a weighted average of out-of-the-money calls and puts, reflecting volatility for the entire S&P 500. Using Bollinger Bands around the VIX can also signal whether the volatility you sell is cheap or expensive. If the price touches the lower end of the Bollinger Band and the working assumption is that volatility reverts to the mean, then you may wait to sell options. If price breaks through the upper Bollinger Band, this might be a great time to sell options, because when volatility reverts to the mean, you can make a quick profit on the move in volatility. This is not a hard-and-fast rule; market conditions may have changed and the VIX may be steadily going down, which is what it did for most of 2009, or perhaps the market is crashing and the VIX is heading in a new direction as it did in 2008. Keep an eye on the VIX as one of many tools in the toolbox for getting a sense of the market.

Another good use of the VIX is to review the VIX's option prices. The cost for an at-the-money put and call should be assumed to be about the same. If you see a big difference between the two, it might be a hint of things to come. If next month's at-the-money prices are substantially higher than this month's, indicating potential large drops in the future, that is another useful hint.

Some indicators are designed to reveal the behavior of buyers and sellers through the flow of money. The indicator developed by Pascal Willain in *Value in Time* (Wiley, 2008) is particularly useful. The Market Profile© is another useful indicator. Instead of expressing price action through a standard graph, it shows you how price is distributed throughout a time period. These types of indicators are used to give you insight as to market behavior and money flow but are not predictive.

Support and resistance lines are very useful but not specifically as support and resistance. They are useful if you consider them as magnets. Markets tend to move quickly to test previous highs and lows. The underlying reason is probably due to the volume of stop and buy orders at round numbers or previous highs or lows. Imagine if the S&P bounced off of 1,100 once before and is now headed in that direction again. There are probably many investors who are short the futures with triggers in place to buy them to close at 1,100, and there are many other sellers ready to sell who think that this time price will fall through support. Whether price falls through support or not, one side is going to make money quickly while the other side will have to quickly cover his position. Either way, it is best to look at support and resistance lines as magnets that can draw price action in a certain direction. After a support line is broken, it tends to become resistance and vice versa. Support and resistance lines also explain why markets tend to move in steps rather than straight lines. Expiration dates for options also influence the market with stock prices moving from strike to strike the closer you get to expiration.

Delta

One of the options trader's favorite tools is Delta, which is also a function of volatility. (Are you starting to see a pattern? Everything is a function of volatility.) To better understand Delta, imagine the probabilities of a single stock trade. If you buy a stock, you have a 50/50 chance that the stock price will move up. Delta for the at-the-money call and put is approximately 50%. Because of this, option traders think of Delta in terms of percentage probabilities as a rule of thumb. Delta represents a degree of value of a contract gaining or losing value for a $1 move. If you buy an at-the-money call with a Delta of .50, then if the stock goes up $1 the value of the contract will go up 50 cents. If it has a Delta of .10, it will go up 10 cents. What Delta will be for any given strike will also depend on current implied volatility. If volatility spikes, a given strike may jump from a Delta of .10 to .20, doubling your risk in a $1 move.

The beauty of Delta is that the market tells you specifically what it thinks are the probabilities of a specific price being reached on expiration day. No technical analysis or fundamental analyses are needed. The prices of the options and resulting "odds" are set by the marketplace. Real traders are putting real money out for options. It is not conjecture or theory. There is no need to seek meaning from a graph or speculate about the Fed's next move. All those concerns and studies are priced into the option. *Delta is the best forward-looking indicator and it is made in real time.* It is not a result of moving averages, support/resistance lines, retracements, waves, cycles, or anything else. It is set by traders. Unfortunately, just being the best indicator does not mean it will be accurate. Delta gives you the market's best guess at a specific point in time.

Delta is not symmetrical between the calls and the puts. Stocks and indexes fall far faster and steeper than they climb. So a strike at Delta 10 should be much further away on the put side than the call side, reflecting the fear that markets make larger moves more quickly on the way down.

Figure 2.1 illustrates both the skews in the Deltas and the effect of volatility on the Deltas. Both examples are from the S&P 500 (SPX), and they both have 28 days until expiration. In the example on the left, the S&P was at 1,212 with the VIX at about 16%. On the right the market was at 883 with a VIX of 77%.

4/23/10 VIX 16%				10/24/08 VIX 77%			
Actuals	**SPX Index**			**Actuals**	**SPX Index**		
	1212.44	+3.77			883.80	-24.20	
Futures	**JUN <56>**			**Futures**	**DEC <56>**		
	1208.50	+6.75			883.80	-31.40	
Options	**MAY <28>**			**Options**	**NOV <28>**		
1275 calls	0.90	11.7%	5.32	1060 calls	8.20	54.4%	7.64
1270 calls	1.10	11.4%	6.98	1055 calls	9.30	55.4%	8.28
1265 calls	1.70	11.8%	9.02	1050 calls	8.00	52.1%	8.95
1260 calls	1.95	11.5%	11.5	1045 calls	11.40	57.1%	9.65
1255 calls	2.50	11.4%	14.3	1040 calls	11.20	55.7%	10.4
1250 calls	3.30	11.6%	17.6	1035 calls	11.90	55.7%	11.1
1245 calls	4.10	11.6%	21.3	1030 calls	13.00	56.3%	11.9
1240 calls	5.60	12.0%	25.4	1025 calls	13.10	55.3%	12.8
1235 calls	6.60	11.9%	29.8	1020 calls	14.90	56.8%	13.6
1175 puts	7.50	15.5%	-20.1	635 puts	10.10	96.1%	-12.6
1170 puts	6.90	16.2%	-17.6	630 puts	9.80	97.0%	-12.2
1165 puts	6.10	16.5%	-15.4	625 puts	9.90	99.2%	-11.7
1160 puts	5.60	17.0%	-13.4	620 puts	9.20	99.0%	-11.3
1155 puts	4.70	17.1%	-11.7	615 puts	8.40	98.3%	-10.9
1150 puts	4.30	17.6%	-10.2	610 puts	8.00	98.8%	-10.5
1145 puts	4.00	18.2%	-8.92	605 puts	8.50	102%	-10.1
1140 puts	3.70	18.8%	-7.79	600 puts	7.70	101%	-9.72

Source: OptionVue 6

FIGURE 2.1   *Comparing condors with equivalent Deltas but different VIX*

The Delta 11 in both cases was not equal distance from the actual price. The distance from the actual price is both quantitatively and qualitatively different. The example on the left represents an extremely calm market, with VIX of 16%; the example on the right, with a VIX of 77%, was of historic proportions. What was the options market telling you?

The market on the left was relatively unconcerned with big moves to the market in either direction. The 1,260 call at Delta 11 was only 48 points (3.9%) away from the actual price, and the 1,155 puts were just 57 points (4.7%) away. Here you see the distance from the price for both the call and put, skewed so that an equivalent Delta 11 on the put side was farther away than the Delta 11 call. This skew is normal because traders know that markets fall faster than they rise; therefore, equivalent Deltas would be different distances from at-the-money options.

It might seem that the market on the left with the lower volatility was telling a completely different story than the market on the right with the higher volatility. After all, on that day the S&P was 883, the Delta 11 calls were at 1,035, and the Delta 11 puts were at 620. The calls were 152 points or 17.2% away from the S&P price. The puts were 29.7% from the price. The options market was telling you that it expected big moves in either direction. So the two markets were dramatically different in terms of what they projected in potential moves. Yet a Delta 11 is a Delta 11. The Delta can change just as market expectations change, so the fact that Delta is the best forward-looking indicator is of limited value for predictive accuracy.

In deciding the position for the wings of your condor, consider the three sources of information: fundamental analysis of the market, charts, and what the options prices reveal about volatility—but not in that order. Always start with what the options are telling you both in the price and in volatility charts. Then examine the charts. Then look at fundamental analysis. Why do you leave fundamental analysis to last? Because this is the least useful criterion for judging market volatility and direction in your limited trading time-frame.

Starting with price, you want your condor to have short strikes as far out as possible. You may focus on the Delta 10 of both the put and call short strikes. A Delta 10 says that a $1 move affects the price by only 10 cents per $1 market move. You can sell under Delta 10, but not too low, is optimal. If you sell Deltas that are too small you end up with too small a credit for both volatility and dollar risk, you will find yourself waiting longer to get the profit you need.

With Delta as your anchor, you can next look at the charts. Will Delta 10 place the short strikes outside some previous lows and highs or other strong support and resistance levels? Is price trending strongly? Is volatility declining or rising? Is institutional money flowing in or out of the market? Is the price moving in or out of the Bollinger Bands? These are some of the basic technical questions to consider when deciding where to place price goals.

Fundamental analysis is probably the last piece of information you need to review. Every trader needs a cursory understanding about why prices might spike.

Was it an unexpected earnings report? Did the Euro crash? Maybe an election result? GDP? Unemployment? All of these and more can cause a sharp move in the stock price, and not necessarily the one you'd expect, but the lasting consequence of news varies greatly. On May 21, 2010, the S&P had one of its worst days ever, dubbed the "flash crash." It dropped 100 points in one day and then bounced back 60 points. You can't look at something like this from a pure volatility and technical point of view. What was the news? Everybody was concerned the euro was going to crash. There may have been a computer problem that created a 60-point swing within 15 minutes. Over the next weekend the E.U. put forward $1 trillion to shore up the Euro and then the market gapped *up* 50 points. You can't always know why these kinds of moves are happening, but you can understand the basic dynamics and effects of volatile market moves.

Price

The third critical piece of information to consider after time and position is the credit you collect for selling your two credit spreads. A condor 200 points wide gives you very different credits if the expiration is 2 weeks from now versus 1 month, 2 months, or longer. The amount of credit you receive is proportional to the amount of risk you are taking.

Credit should be evaluated of as a percentage of total margin at risk. For example, you are using $10,000 as margin to sell your condor and you receive a credit of $1,000. If you keep the condor through expiration and it expires worthless, you keep the $1,000. If the price expires outside the wings, you might give up the $10,000 but keep the $1,000 so, technically, you are risking only $9,000. Think of credit as a percentage of total margin and ignore the credit you receive as a mitigating factor in risk. You have no intention of keeping the entire credit anyway, and what you are interested in is what kind of return you make for the margin you are putting at risk.

Since you are going to examine trading the SPX, you also need to know how far apart the strikes should be for each spread. For instance, if you sell a call at 1,200, which call do you buy? The 1,205 or the 1,210, for example? A popular approach is to buy the next strike out, or the 1,205.

With the SPX the greatest liquidity is found at the strikes every quarter step, meaning 1,200, 1,225, 1,250, and 1,275, for example. The greater the liquidity, the tighter the bid-ask spread.

Another advantage to trading the quarter strikes is less obvious. When you enter the trade when the market is at a quarter strike, you will find it easier to balance the Deltas when your short strikes are also at quarter strikes. This one observation allows you to take your time before entering a trade rather than jumping in too quickly or at the wrong price point. The SPX has a tendency to gravitate to these prices precisely because of the greater liquidity in options, futures, and ETFs. Since everybody is more interested in these prices, you may be too. You will want to trade with the institutions in this case and not against them.

So if you sell a single spread on the SPX consisting of short 1,200 calls and long 1,225 calls, the margin on that spread is $2,500. An identically spaced spread sold on the put side, such as short 1,000 puts and long 975 puts, requires the same $2,500 margin. You may be able to use the same $2,500 to margin both spreads.[2] With the index options this makes sense. Since they are European-style options and can be exercised only at expiration, the price can "lose" only on one side of the condor or the other.

What strikes will you trade and how far apart should they be in order to have a consistent basis in price? Every $0.25 credit you receive for selling your condor is equivalent to 1% return on margin. Therefore, $1 is 4% credit, and $2 is equal to an 8% credit.

Knowing in advance what kind of return you expect is crucial in determining what kind of credit you need to receive to start out. If you wanted a return of 4% on the trade, and you sold a condor for $4, you would "buy" back the condor at $3 and keep $1, making 4%. In this example the condor would have to decay only 25% in value to move from $4 to $3. What if you sold the condor for $2? Then it would have to lose 50% in value in order to get the desired return. If your goal is to expose yourself to the market as little as possible, you would want the position that will decay the quickest to achieve your goal.

---

2. *Review your broker's margin policies.*

Putting It Together

A condor decision is based on time, position, and price. How far are you trading from expiration, which strikes are you selling and buying, and what credit are you hoping to earn in order to achieve your return on margin? The following is the best of each condition:

- *Position:* The Delta 10s are well outside previous highs and lows. Charts are not trending strongly in either direction. The news is good and everybody is happy.

- *Price:* You could get a high credit of $5 for this trade equal to 20% of margin. Volatility, which has been trending nicely on the downside, just had a 1-day spike.

- *Time:* Expiration is in 4 to 5 weeks.

The reason this particular setup is difficult is that the objectives can be mutually exclusive.

Choice #1: If you want a *short expiration window,* you usually sacrifice position or price. The shorter the time until expiration, the smaller the condor becomes. Or you can have the Delta 10 and the short expiration, but you probably won't get your credit goal.

Choice #2: If *position* is your main concern and the Deltas have to be 10, the problems are switched around. You can have Delta 10 and the short expiration but will probably have to sacrifice the high credit. Delta 10s might be possible with the high credit but not in the short expiration.

Choice #3: The last scenario is insisting on a *high credit* when selling your condor. A high credit is possible in a short expiration but not with the strikes so far away at Delta 10. You can still obtain a high credit with Delta 10s, but you will probably have to give up on a short expiration.

The constraints placed on the trade created the situation in which obtaining all three conditions is difficult if not impossible. You need to prioritize what you want in the trade. This defines what is most important to you.

Any of the above strategies is fine. Each has strengths and weaknesses. If you want the Delta 10s and rapid time decay, you may trade anywhere from 3 to 5 weeks from expiration. You might conclude that the best approach is to start with price, then look at position, and finally look at time.

Price is your first consideration because you want to capture a portion of the credit but not all of it. Keeping one-third or one-quarter of the credit is much easier than waiting long enough to capture half of the credit. The object is to make money and get out of the position as soon as possible.

Position is, therefore, directed by price. If the position is at Delta 10s and it can't provide a minimum credit, you need to either wait until it does or trade the farther-out month. Position is also nonnegotiable.

Time is negotiable. The market doesn't care about your condor. If your range is too narrow because you wanted short time decay or a bigger credit, the market will have no mercy. Time is the only constant in trading condors. When things go wrong, time works against you if there is not enough of it left. Consider keeping a "reserve" of time in your trade so that you have enough of it to make adjustments if necessary. Your "account" of time will deplete, so make sure you have enough and use it wisely.

Since this is a time-decay strategy at heart, why is time your final consideration and not your first? Time is a two-edged sword. You are asking the market to remain relatively stable for a number of weeks. The sought-after stability can be met with a sharp move in the market in one direction or the other. When sharp moves occur, you want to be able to adjust your condor to conform to the new reality and protect your principal. The ability to adjust is a luxury derived from additional time. The larger window of time remaining until expiration also allows you to decide *when* to remove or adjust your trade. As expiration looms, your timetable for making a decision dwindles and the market makes you either remove the trade for a potential loss or stay through expiration.

Why Enter a Trade?

There is one more consideration: What is your reason to enter a trade? Why do you want to sell a condor? Are you seeking monthly returns? Are you looking for the shortest trade possible? Are you looking for the highest returns possible? Your motivation will determine the "why" of entering a trade.

If your motivation is monthly returns, don't trade at all. You can't force the market to give you monthly returns, but you can try to take advantage of every expiration period to sell a condor. In this scenario you look for a window of time of 6 to 12 weeks out from expiration. A relatively large down day is an excellent opportunity to take advantage of higher prices and sell from the increase in volatility. It is always better to trade out of opportunity, not necessity.

A good strategy, therefore, is to enter a trade is to wait for a jump in implied volatility measured by the VIX. The premise behind this entry is that volatility will revert to the mean, so you can take advantage of the drop in Vega and make a quick profit. This is not the same strategy as time decay. The goal here is to make a volatility trade. If it fails, the volatility trade can revert to a time-decay trade. The Vega effect will be largest the farther out in time the trade is from expiration, but going out too far in time is risky because further increases in volatility can work sharply against you.

There are different ways to measure a significant jump in the VIX:

- The jump can be in percentage terms relative to the previous day. So you can set a rule that you will sell a condor only if the VIX jumps 10%, 20%, or 30%. Where you set this bar determines how frequently you trade.

- You can set your standard as a break in the upper Bollinger Band on the VIX, which, in a stable market, could be a much smaller number than the percentage guideline. If the market has been calm, breaking the upper Bollinger Band may not be that useful.

- The third approach is to measure the standard deviation in the change in the price of the VIX or the S&P and decide to sell only if the change is greater than 2 standard deviations.

- The best entry is found when a combination of the preceding factors converge at the same time.

In Figure 2.2, a spike in the price and the VIX through their Bollinger Bands marked a turnaround for both the VIX and the S&P. The spike in the bottom part of each chart was measured in standard deviations, so both the VIX and the S&P moved more than 2 standard deviations relative to previous price moves. They also broke the Bollinger Bands in both charts, more than 2 standard deviations from the 20-day moving average.

The S&P moved from 1,040 to 1,100 within 10 days, which is 5.8%, while the VIX dropped from 31 to 23, a 25.8% drop in volatility. Gains made from drops in volatility like this almost always outpace losses from the quick move in price. That advantage can evaporate if you wait too long and the price continues to rise; then you become a victim of Gamma.

These volatility rules are less concerned with a specific number of days to expiration as the determining factor for entering a trade, and more focused on volatility as the buzzer for entry. You may have to be quick on the trigger to make this work optimally. A trading day may start with a great deal of volatility at the open, blow through Bollinger Bands and show a statistically significant price move, and then wilt away after the first half-hour of trading.

VIX: BB and Statistical Spike

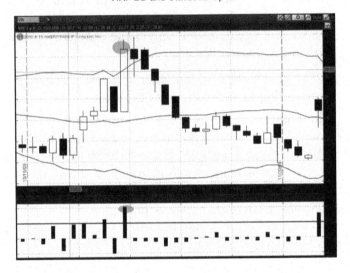

S&P: BB and Statistical Spike

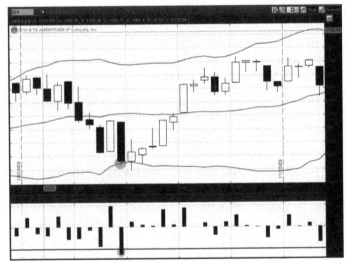

Source: thinkorswim by TD Ameritrade

FIGURE 2.2   *VIX and S&P spikes*

Indecisiveness or hesitation leads to lost opportunity. If you wait to see whether more volatility will enter the market, hoping for a better price, it might be a long wait. The old cliché that you can't time the market is not just true, but absolutely and completely true. If you get the best price through timing, you were probably just lucky. If you know what price you want in advance and you get it, you have to recognize that it was good enough and move on.

Rules for Putting on a Trade

Patiently waiting to put on a trade allows you the luxury of being choosy. There is no requirement to get into a trade, so use the flexibility to choose a trade that has a high probability of success but also reflects your own risk profile. Regardless of the trigger you use to enter a trade, you still need a set of rules to guide your condor decisions, keeping in mind all the issues in play. What follows is one set of rules for putting on a trade that has worked in good times and bad:

1. Get a minimum of $3 credit or greater for the trade, which is 12% return on margin. The smaller the credit you start with, the longer you will need to be in the market to get the return you expect.

2. Deltas should be 10 or less if possible but never greater than 12. You may be tempted to look at the charts, eyeball support and resistance, and set your condor accordingly. Don't do it. Believe what the options market is telling you. If the market reveals that a price has a Delta of 10 and another has a delta of 18, don't think the price will never get to

the 18 level. Because of the nature of Delta, the potential losses will also grow very quickly.

3. Expiration day must be no closer than 49 days. If volatility takes a huge jump before day 42, consider it, but prefer to trade the month farther out.

4. The call short strikes should be at least 100 to 125 points higher than the current price, and the put short strikes should be at least 125 points lower. These numbers put a straightjacket around the other conditions. In volatile markets where sudden large moves are not completely out of the ordinary, if you have well over 100 points in each direction, you build in a cushion. Some people have said, "The market will never move 150 points." That's not the point. You don't even want to get close to your short strikes. If you are within 50 points, you need to consider adjusting your position.[3]

5. Trade when the SPX is at a quarter price. This is a constraint that helps your trade. It balances Deltas since your strikes are also at quarter prices. If the S&P is at 1,115, Deltas are not balanced the way you'd like and you don't have a good sense of which way the market will be going. When the S&P reaches a quarter point price, there is a good chance that the price will be revisited even if it shoots through it.

6. Get in on a day when the volatility is spiking up (that is, a down day).

---

3. *By the way, these size condors will obviously need to be reassessed if the S&P settles in the 600s again or if the volatility drops to 10 or lower, but you get the idea.*

It is always better to consider the state of the market you are selling into. However, you can still trade options profitably without knowing anything about the market. Since you are merely "trading the math," all you need to know are the Greeks and your P&L. The length and strength of trends give you valuable information when you're placing your condor trade.

There is no back-testing for this strategy because you are using a method rather than a programmed reaction trade. Your risk tolerance defines how you trade. No two people should make exactly the same trade because their risk tolerance will not be the same.

The market will be in one of three directions: up, down, or sideways. By the time you can clearly spot a trend, it might be over. However, you can't ignore an obvious trend. So what do you do in different markets?

Sideways Market

A sideways market is the most profitable for a condor trader. Moving sideways means that the market moves within the range of your condor while you are in the trade, preferably closest to the midpoint. Depending on how you placed your trade, the market may or may not be moving sideways for you, however. If the S&P over the past month has been moving in a 50-point range and you sell a condor whose VIX is based on that trend, then all is fine as long as the range stays within the 50 points. On the other hand, if the market becomes more volatile and the range is now 100 points, as far as you are concerned it is no longer moving sideways. If you sold a condor when the market was at this new 100-point range, the market was moving sideways for your condor.

So a "sideways" market is relative only to the condor you placed and the volatility circumstance you found yourself in.

The longer the market has moved sideways, the more suspicious you should be about continued calm going forward. Consider what you expect from the market. You want extended stability to be rewarded with more stability. Markets are inherently unstable, so by asking for even greater stability, you are hoping for the market to remain stable beyond what might be reasonable. This is the main reason for staying in the market as short a time as possible. It often occurs that the greatest stability is followed by a big move as the market tries to figure out what to do next. If you are fortunate enough to get the stability you need in a short timeframe to make a profit, take it and don't push your luck.

Uptrending Market

If the market is trending upward, you may notice continuing falling volatility. That is the good news. The bad news is that an aggressive up market can be difficult to adjust. So up is good but up too fast is not good.

Uptrending markets are the scariest and most difficult to trade. There is always the fear that the day after you enter the trade the market will take a sharp downturn and volatility will work strongly against you, so you may hesitate to put in the trade. This trepidation is why it is best to wait until a down move in the market if possible. You want drops in volatility to work for you to hedge against rapid up moves, or Gamma, in the market.

A few more words about what volatility is not. It is important not to confuse volatility with large fluctuations in the market, even though that is generically how volatility is usually understood. A 3% *drop* in the market might cause volatility to spike up 10%. A 3% *jump* in the market does not necessarily cause a similar drop in the volatility, even though it is an equally volatile move strictly in terms of price movement. Volatility is more a measure of fear about how much the market could move *down,* not up. A down move in an up market is one of the best trades.

In the example shown in Figure 2.3, from July 2009, you see that the S&P moved from 880 to 1,000, which is a 13.6% increase in the market where the market didn't break a new low for more than a month. The VIX, on the other hand, bounced from 26 to 23, then back to 26. The inverse correlation between the VIX and the S&P fell apart as the market rose. The stability in the VIX showed that nobody trusted the rally. Many condor sellers lost money in this trade waiting too long for the correction that didn't come and getting no help from shrinking volatility.

Figure 2.4 shows the reverse scenario.

Rising Market

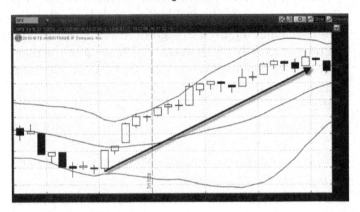

Flat VIX

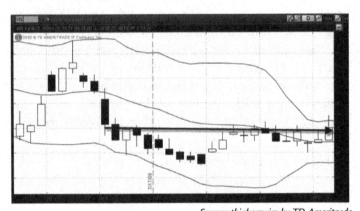

FIGURE 2.3   *Comparing a rising market to a flat VIX*

Falling Market

Rising VIX

Source: thinkorswim by TD Ameritrade

FIGURE 2.4   *Relationship between a falling market and a rising VIX*

In the beginning of 2009, the S&P dropped from 920 to 800, a 13% drop. The VIX jumped from 37 to 57, a 54% increase. So volatility may be a good indicator of how much further the market might move down because of the premiums buyers are willing to pay, but volatility is far less useful for how far a market could move up.

So in an uptrending market be very careful to leave an overexuberant market enough room to continue its exuberance. Looking at the Greeks just might not be enough. Never say the market "can't" do something, as in, "It can't go any higher," because one day it will.

When the market goes up and up, you might want to wait for the market to finish another leg up to the next quarter price before selling. If the market can't make it and falls back to the lower quarter price, you can use the lower quarter price as a reference point. The long-expected big down day with the spike in the VIX might not happen for quite some time. This is why it can sometimes be good to lean on the quarter prices as points of entry. Although the preference is to get in on a down day, this may not happen for quite some time in an up market. The key is to assume that the trend will continue; but also assume that the market could just as easily give it all up at once.

Another important consideration in an up market is not the trend or strength of the price movement, but the trend and strength of volatility. In an up market volatility is probably decreasing, which is good for the condor trade. But just how far down is the VIX? Is the VIX progressively falling from historic highs as it did in 2009, or is it trading from yearly lows as it did in early 2010?

So the question is, how much lower can volatility reasonably fall? Pay attention to the level of the VIX and how it is trending.

Don't be misled into thinking that low volatility instantly discounts the possibility of trading. The key is not whether volatility is low. The most important issue is whether implied volatility is still higher than statistical volatility.

In early 2010, implied volatility on the S&P was around 15 but statistical volatility was around 9. So the implied volatility priced into the options was still higher than actual volatility. Options sellers, in spite of the extremely low volatility, were still making money in this extremely low-volatility environment. Of course, that situation couldn't last forever and it didn't. Note the arrows in Figure 2.5 and how quickly the gap between implied and statistical volatility was filled. If you choose to trade in that kind of environment, be ready to get out of the trade as quickly as you can to make a profit.

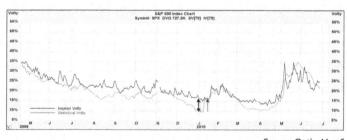

Source: OptionVue 6

FIGURE 2.5   *Gap between implied and statistical volatility*

Downtrending Market

In a downtrending market, you don't want to get in too soon. You want to sell at a volatility peak if possible. Of course, you can't time the market. When a market starts to fall, there is always the possibility of a sharp rebound. The ideal situation is provided by a spike in the VIX in standard deviation and a break in the Bollinger Bands. There are no guarantees, and a large move just might be a prelude to another larger move—but there are no perfect entry points, just good ones.

Shape of the Curve

The natural inclination is to seek to place a trade when the current price is equidistant from both wings, 125 points in both directions, for example. This makes the condor a genuinely market-neutral trade. But that does not make it a Delta-neutral trade, which is truly directionally neutral from an options perspective. Following the rules of trading at the quarter strikes and at Delta 10 gives you an advantageous P&L graph for changing conditions in the market.

In the example shown in Figure 2.6, a condor was sold with 825/850 puts and 1,125/1,150 calls with Deltas of approximately 10.

Figure 2.7 shows what the P&L is for this trade. The little black ball resting on the dotted zero line represents the price and value of the condor at entry, $0. Immediately after you sold the condor, if the market went up the position started to lose value. If the market price goes down, the ball travels up the curve and gains value. This model assumes that volatility remains exactly the same throughout.

Options	AUG <49>			
	MktPr	MIV	Trade	Delta
1250 calls				
1225 calls	0.20	20.8%		0.05
1200 calls	0.30	19.7%		0.38
1175 calls	0.45	18.7%		1.67
1150 calls	1.45	19.9%	+10	4.85
1125 calls	3.40	20.8%	-10	10.5
1100 calls	7.50	22.2%		18.6
900 puts	12.00	35.8%		-16.4
875 puts	9.00	37.4%		-12.7
850 puts	6.70	39.0%	-10	-9.71
825 puts	5.00	40.7%	+10	-7.42
800 puts	3.70	42.3%		-5.66
775 puts	2.65	43.7%		-4.32
750 puts	1.95	45.5%		-3.29

Source: OptionVue 6

FIGURE 2.6   *Delta 10 condor*

Reality gives you a different picture. What if the market went down 2% and volatility went up 2%? The curve would shift downward but the ball would still be moving up the curve. Figure 2.8 shows that the net effect is break-even although the market went down and the volatility went up.

On the other hand, if the market moved up 2%, you might expect volatility to drop 2%. The curve in Figure 2.9 shows that the condor should be showing a loss as the S&P went up in price because the ball would move down the curve. However as volatility drops, the curve moves up, providing a hedge against loss as the S&P rose.

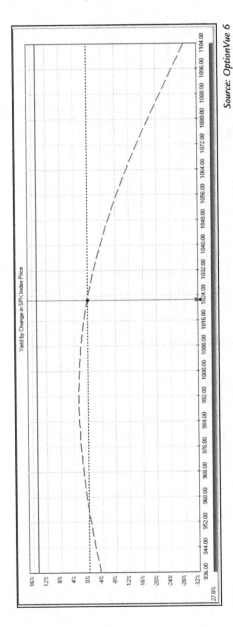

Source: OptionVue 6

FIGURE 2.7   *Graph of condor when value is at $0*

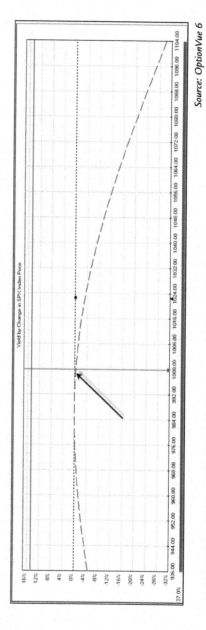

FIGURE 2.8 *P&L curve drops when IV goes up and still at breakeven*

Source: OptionVue 6

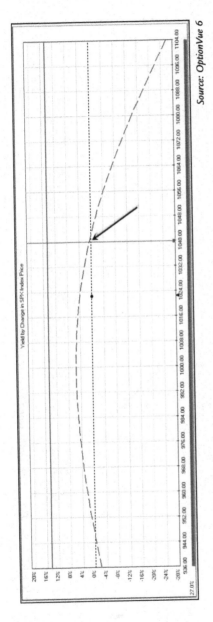

Source: OptionVue 6

FIGURE 2.9   *P&L curve rises when IV drops and still at breakeven*

Placing your trade so that price is in the precise middle of the condor puts you at a disadvantage during another down move. On the other hand, decreasing volatility should cover you in a rising market as well. Because of this dynamic, properly placed trades frequently stay positive throughout the life of the trade.

Options are best understood three-dimensionally, with changes in time, price, and volatility. Graphs are two-dimensional but the addition of volatility produces a variety of possible graphs. Good options software allows you to tweak different scenarios to analyze all the possibilities.

In the next chapter, these rules are applied in the best and worst markets.

Chapter 3

Trading Journal

Using the built-in probabilities associated with Deltas, any generic condor with wings that is stretched far enough will usually make money. Some traders sell condors and just let them sit through expiration simply because of their high probability of profit. They also accept that they'll get blown out once in a while, but the money they put at risk is so small that they don't care, as long as the gains exceed the losses.

The managed approach proposed in this book is a completely different animal. There are other ways to increase the probabilities. The first is to patiently wait for the right opportunity to enter a trade. Let a trend run its course and wait for the market to settle down. An appreciation and deeper understanding of volatility will also increase your odds of success because the probabilities can be misleading. Finally, there is no better way to increase the probability for success than to claim a profit when the opportunity presents itself. Profit is the very definition of a successful trade.

The temptation with condors is to wait that one extra day or week to squeeze out even more profit. Almost every trade you exit could possibly do better, perhaps even twice as well, sometimes for just an extra day or two. On the other hand, you might watch profits evaporate into losses and then find yourself scrambling to make defensive adjustments that add weeks to your trade. It is for those few trades that could have really been dangerous that you should be cautious with the rest. There is no point in making a return of 40% if you are going to lose 50% or 100% in a single trade. A good rule of thumb: Don't try to stare down the market because the market never blinks.

What separates the winners from the losers is the exit strategy. The exit strategy that works best is to give back *almost* all of the credit. If you take in an initial 16% credit and keep only 3%, 4%, or 5%, you're giving back most of the potential profits. How many trades have you made that can consistently make profits of 3% in a few days regardless of the direction of the market?

Staying Through Expiration

So why not stay through expiration? One reason is Gamma. Think of Gamma as a slide, and the steeper the slider, the quicker you lose money. Gamma can turn the trade against you very quickly.

In the scenario illustrated in Figure 3.1, there were only 5 days left until expiration. The market was at 1,090 and there was a 9% profit for closing the position. Held until expiration, the credit would be 15%. If price moved up 10 points, the position would be worthless. If it moved up 20 points, the position would be worth –10%. If that happened, you would be within 15 points of your short strikes, and with only 5 days left to go, you could lose it all.

This is a generous example because volatility didn't change. The positive effects of decreasing volatility during expiration week are meaningless when you are close to your strikes. In fact, the price will act as though volatility increased rather than decreased even though the market is moving up because of the intense buying pressure on the call side.

Markets usually drop faster than they rise, so what do you think would happen if the market dropped suddenly? Volatility goes up, the P&L curve drops, and the slide goes way down as depicted in Figure 3.1. The theoretical models on these graphs don't show the reality. Instead of being down 10%, you could be down 30%, 40%, or more.

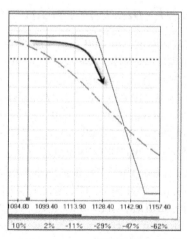

Source: OptionVue 6

FIGURE 3.1   *Gamma slide*

Remember, when you are closing a condor you are a buyer. The shoe is now on the other foot. If the market is crashing, the seller is going to take advantage of the situation and not sell his options cheaply. The seller knows that time is against you the buyer and your choices are limited. You don't want to be in that situation if you can avoid it.

The other reason is that you are now completely a victim to the market and time is no longer your ally. Time decay increases rapidly in expiration week, but if the market breaks through one of your strikes and stays there, all that potential time decay will mean nothing. There are no defensive strategies such as adjusting spreads this late in the game. You either take a loss or pray the market will move in your direction. Prayer as a risk management strategy is really the subject of another book.

Expiration Friday

There is a misconception that stock options settle on an expiration price on the closing bell on Friday. They don't. They actually settle on Saturday. Stocks continue trading in the aftermarket after the market closes; the price can still move rapidly. You can't trade options anymore after the closing bell, so if there is any news in the aftermarkets, you are potentially a victim.

With indexes like the SPX it is potentially worse. The last time you can trade the SPX is at 4:15 PM ET on the Thursday of expiration week. However, the SPX does not settle with a closing price until Friday. When on Friday? Well, there is the rub. All the component companies on the S&P have to start trading before they can have a settlement number for options expiration. That's 500 companies. Settlement can take a half an hour or more after the opening bell. This means that whatever options you sold are at the mercy of news and market forces from 4:15 PM ET Thursday to whenever they have a settlement number on Friday. By the way, you can usually see this effect on the Friday of expiration week. Watch how the market frequently will charge in one direction at the open and then reverse sharply half an hour later. This is not a coincidence. With the Russell 2000 (RUT), settlement can take all day. Imagine waiting all day to find out whether your calls are in-the-money or out-of-the-money.

Parameters for Exiting a Trade

Exiting a trade is where you make money. Unrealized gains and losses don't mean a thing. If you can spend it, it's yours; otherwise, it's not. Only four considerations should guide your exit strategy.

The first consideration is profit. After you decide how much profit you are shooting for, you can make a hard and fast rule to exit with that profit. In fact, the best thing you can do is place a limit order to buy to close the condor at a specific price that is good until cancelled (GTC) immediately after you open the condor. If you make the decision in advance, you prevent yourself from staying in the trade too long.

The trading experience is less stressful if you place limit orders in advance. Many traders make the mistake of not knowing exactly what they want. Indecision means that you are making decisions all the time. Every tick of the market becomes a decision. Should I get out now? Or now? Or now? Indecision itself is a decision, just the wrong one.

Place the order before the open if the market looks as though it is moving in your favor. Some traders call the first half-hour of trading "amateur hour." Maybe this is true for stock traders who get snookered into jumping onto a quick trend, but for option traders who are trading Theta, Delta, Gamma, and Vega, it is an opportunity for both entry and exit.

The second consideration is time left until expiration. Buy to close the condor approximately a month before expiration, as a general standard. This is, of course, the exact opposite of how most condor traders trade. They like to sell 1 month before expiration. The difference is that your condors may be substantially larger in size between the wings, which grants a far better defensive position in case of a sudden move in the market. You may also exit the trade when you want to and not because you have one eye on the expiration calendar. If you do need to stay in the trade longer because the market moves against you, rapid time decay in the final month becomes your ally.

The third consideration is knowing where you are on the P&L curve. Are you at break-even? Or at midpoint? Take your profits when the position moves from break-even into the profit zone. Don't hesitate. Price can move into a profitable position and then move back out sharply. You'll always be disappointed that you didn't make more money because you got out too early. That is just human nature. But that disappointment doesn't compare to kicking yourself for not getting out for a profit when the position started to go negative. You can never go broke taking a profit.

The final but most important consideration is capital preservation. When you're selling a condor, your objective is, of course, to make money. If during the course of the trade you have to adjust the whole position because the market is moving against you, your first priority is to close the trade at break-even if possible. There also has to be a point of no return in terms of loss and time. How long will you wait to take a 10% loss? Or 15%? More? Adjustments can be made to protect your condor position, but sometimes even those don't work. You can't get it right every time and you have to be prepared to take an occasional loss. If you insist on being profitable 100% of the time, you will eventually lose everything. A lot of small gains and an occasional small loss are the keys to success over the long run.

Adjustments

The values of both sides of a condor behave as if on a seesaw. When the market crashes down, the value of the put spread inflates quickly and the value of the call spread dissipates just as quickly. The problem you run into is that a call spread that drops in value can fall only to zero, whereas the price of the put spread can go up much higher than the call spread can go down.

Journal of Actual Trades

Enough theory. Now let's turn to actual trades executed by the author of this book in which things went right and things went wrong. Since the market was extremely unbalanced during the years 2008–2010, you don't have to go far to cover the kaleidoscope of easy and difficult trades. Some studies suggest that the recent increased participation of High Frequency Traders may have added to market volatility in that period, so a volatile market is a better guide for examination in any case. As you go through the trades, you will find out how to protect your principal and make a profit.

The Perfect Trade

Unfortunately, the perfect trade can't be identified until after the trade is finished, but you can look for optimal conditions. So what would a perfect trade have looked like? You would have seen the market move sideways as well as diminishing volatility. This combination results in large returns in a short period after you enter the trade.

Sideways Market

The time was December 2009. Assume that you had recently exited a trade in November and were looking for an opportunity to enter the market. You were looking for a drop in the market to take advantage of a jump in volatility. Figure 3.2 shows the charts worth looking at.

You would have been eager to get back in the market quickly for December because of the holidays and the end of the year. All those vacation days are also included in time decay, so you wouldn't want to miss out on the opportunity. The VIX chart shows that you might have missed out on a good opportunity to take advantage of a spike in the VIX when it gapped up. However, you might have wanted to see whether there would be any follow-through the next day, which never occurred. Finally, on December 8, when the market dropped a bit and VIX rose to 24, you could have sold a February condor for a credit of 18% on margined capital.

SPX

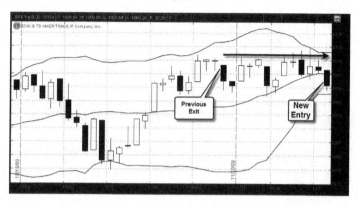

VIX

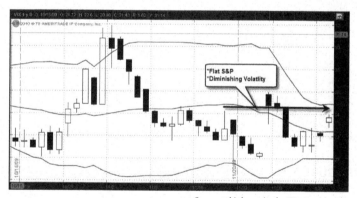

Source: thinkorswim by TD Ameritrade

FIGURE 3.2   *Sideways S&P and sideways VIX*

The set-up is great as described; however, the execution was less than desirable. Why? Looking at Figure 3.3, you see that the puts were sold at a Delta of 17.4 instead of 10, breaking one of your rules of trading Delta 10 or less, and your calls were sold at a Delta of 7. The market had been on a tear since the March lows of 666, and you would have been more concerned about the call side than the put side. You would also have expected traders to start discounting ahead of the holidays, thereby dropping the implied volatility and price of the options.

Options	FEB <73>					
1375 calls	MktPr	MIV	Trade	Ex.Pos	Delta	OrigPr
1350 calls	0.40	21.0%			0.06	.....
1325 calls	0.95	22.0%			0.23	.....
1300 calls	0.55	18.5%			0.69	.....
1275 calls	0.75	17.7%			1.74	.....
1250 calls	1.45	17.8%	+4		3.78	.....
1225 calls	2.85	18.1%	-4		7.23	.....
1200 calls	5.10	18.3%			12.4	.....
1175 calls	9.50	19.2%			19.3	.....
1025 puts	22.70	25.1%			-28.2	.....
1000 puts	17.50	26.5%			-22.2	.....
975 puts	13.70	27.9%	-4		-17.4	.....
950 puts	10.60	29.3%	+4		-13.6	.....
925 puts	7.90	30.4%			-10.6	.....
900 puts	6.00	31.7%			-8.25	.....
875 puts	4.50	33.0%			-6.44	.....
850 puts	3.80	35.1%			-5.03	.....

Source: OptionVue 6

FIGURE 3.3　*Condor trade with high Delta on the puts*

Some traders call weekends and holidays "free days" because you get the benefits of time decay without any trading going on. Unfortunately, there is no free ride. If a big event happens over the weekend, which is usually the case if there is some government intervention, the market will price in 2 or 3 days' worth of news right at the open after the holiday. So those days are not free. The only edge you have, and this is a very important edge, is buying to close condors *right before the long weekend* when the Theta decay is discounted from the price of the options. Prices will start to decline after about midday on Fridays or the day prior to the holidays and will be likely to drop quickly in the final few minutes of the trading day, in particular the 15 minutes after 4 PM. On the other hand, the time decay over long weekends is a good reason to try to sell condors at least two to three days before the holidays and before the long weekend starts lowering option prices.

You may look for an opportunity to buy to close your condor within 2 to 4 weeks after selling it and at least a month before expiration. Looking at Figure 3.4, you see that in 18 days you would be well within your other goal of 4% profit. Of course, this is merely a theoretical model and anything could happen, but at least you have a sense of what the trade looks like going forward.

Conditions turned out to be perfect. The market continued to move sideways, which is always beneficial for a condor. Additionally, the VIX dropped from 24 to 20. In Figure 3.4, the most profit predicted in the theoretical model after 18 days is 6%. Instead, as depicted in Figure 3.5, 12 days later on December 20, you buy to close the condor and pocket an 8% profit. How was that possible? The third dimension of the chart not portrayed in the two-dimensional chart is volatility. Declining volatility shifted the P&L curves up, creating higher and quicker returns.

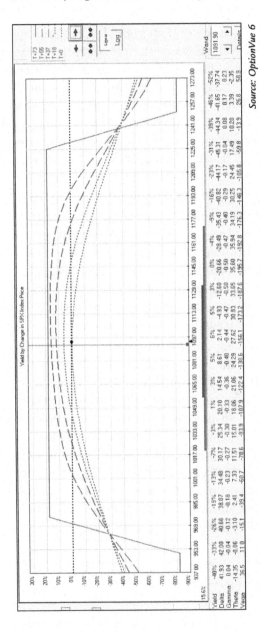

FIGURE 3.4   *73-day condor*

Source: OptionVue 6

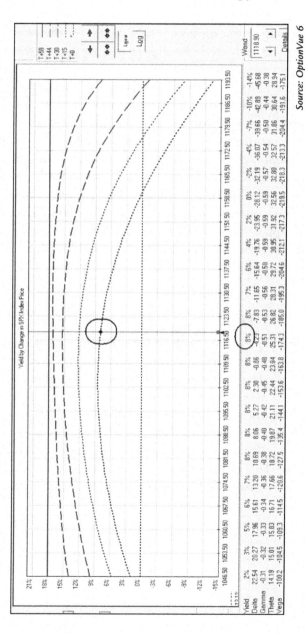

FIGURE 3.5 *Accelerated profits from drop in implied volatility*

The next question is, why not stay in the position? There were a bunch of holidays coming up and the market would be closed. Use the days off for additional time decay dollars. In retrospect (always in retrospect), you could have stayed in and made more money. But you locked in an 8% gain in 12 days. This captured 44% of all the profit possible in this condor. When you entered the condor, there were 73 days until expiration and getting out in 12 days meant you were in the trade for only 16% of the life of the condor. Why expose yourself to continuing market risk? On those holidays big events can happen (remember the Berlin Wall falling?) that can also leave you vulnerable. Those are not free days. Also, nobody complains when they make a profit.

Great Trade in a Down Market

Figure 3.6 shows a trade in which you could stay pretty close to your rules. On June 29, 2010, the S&P drops by 3%. The VIX jumps from 29 to 35, about 20%. There is also an over 2 standard deviation spike in both the VIX and the SPX. The S&P drops to 1,045. You sell an August condor 875/900 puts (150 points away) and 1,175/1,200 (125 points away) with 52 days until expiration. The Delta on the 900 is 13 and on the 1,175 about 7. Always give yourself room for a reversal.

SPX

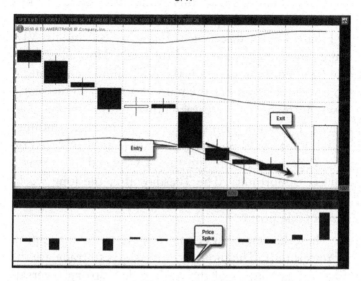

VIX

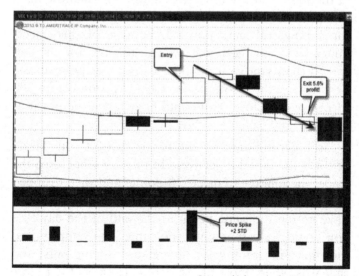

FIGURE 3.6   *Declining market and a declining VIX*

A few factors make this trade successful, the key being an unusual drop in volatility. In the charts shown in Figure 3.6, the direction of both the S&P and the VIX were down after you entered the trade. Normally, when the S&P continues to fall, the VIX should continue to go up, especially since the market goes on to hit yearly lows. Instead, the VIX goes down as the market goes down. The condor gains value as the market continues to fall another 30 points. This trade was also placed on the Wednesday before the July 4 weekend, so it was a perfect opportunity. The Tuesday after the long weekend, the market rallies at the open. You make a very respectable profit.

The other factor was entering the trade at the peak of uncertainty. The most unstable times to trade are the first and last hours of the trading day. Strong reversals in the first hour are not uncommon. So when the market opens strongly down, there is always the possibility for a powerful snap upward. Because of this uncertainty, you can receive a great deal more for the call spread than you would have at any other point in the day. In fact, the position was already profitable by 1% to 2% by the close. You could have taken the profit at the close and called it a day.

Still, getting out as soon as you can get your target profit is the initial objective. On the day you closed the trade, the market went up 20 points and then dropped all the way back down, in which case you could not have gotten the same profit at the end of the day that you could have that same morning. The jump-started morning rally took a lot of pressure off the puts, and that was where most of the profits came as their price went down. When the rally failed, those put prices went right back up. If you had not gotten out of the trade on that day, you would have been kicking yourself, especially if the market continued to drop the next day. As it was, the market went straight up for the next 6 days. Hindsight is easy. The market usually punishes you for predicting.

Actually, trades that happen in the first hour of the day can produce the fastest profits. Economic data usually comes out 1 hour before the market opens or a half hour after it opens. The full impact of the news that comes out 1 hour before the market opens is largely digested by the time the market opens. If there is bad news, you can try to take advantage of obvious volatility before the market calms down. If it is good news, you can try to grab a profit before the market changes its mind. If you miss the first hour you frequently have missed your opportunity.

Not-So-Pretty Trade

The one disadvantage of waiting for a jump in volatility as a signal for selling condors is that not infrequently the spike is the beginning of a new upward climb in trader fear. There is no way of knowing that from the beginning, and sometimes you just get caught.

On January 15, 2010, a new entry point to sell condors appeared. You had closed your previous position on December 22 and had already waited almost a month for an opportunity. Actually, the previous market moves looked very kindly toward condors. The S&P had moved up slowly from 1,114 from your previous position to 1,133. Figure 3.7 shows what the VIX chart looked like.

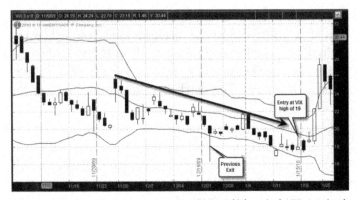

Source: thinkorswim by TD Ameritrade

FIGURE 3.7   *Trading a declining before a spike*

You sell your condor when the VIX jumps from 15 to 19, which seemed like a lot at the time. The feeling that this was a large move is confirmed by the jump in implied volatility from the teens to the twenties, creating a new beneficial gap with statistical volatility, as depicted in Figure 3.8. So the trade looked pretty good. You sell March 975/1,000 puts and 1,275/1,300 calls with 63 days left for a 14% credit with 63 days until expiration. The Deltas for the calls were 10 and for the puts 11.

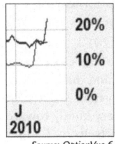

Source: OptionVue 6

FIGURE 3.8   *Volatility gap*

In the next 4 trading days, the VIX jumps from 19 to 28, a 30% increase, with the S&P falling to 1,095. You start thinking it might be a good time to raise more credit in case the put spread needs to be bought and resold at a lower strike. So you pay $0.50 to buy to close the call spread that you had sold for $2, pocketing $1.50 credit, and sell the 1,200/1,225 call spread for an additional $1.35. The Deltas on the 1,200 were only 6, so even if you rolled down the calls 50 points, the options market was telling you that there still was not that much risk in it.

Move forward less than a week to January 28, and the S&P falls further to a low of 1,085 and the VIX rises to a high of 26. The big news that moved the market was fear of Greece defaulting and damaging the euro. This is the kind of news that is the most worrisome. It was not just a company or a sector but a whole major currency at stake. Your condor didn't look as though it was built for that kind of market, which was clearly reflected in the damage the increase in the VIX was doing to it. The market looked as though it wanted to keep going down. You wisely decide to put an order to close the trade at break-even and unintentionally make a profit of .5% on the whole trade. "Live to fight another day" is an acceptable strategy.

The *very next day* the market fell some more, and you jump right back in and sell the March 925/950 (11 Delta) puts and the 1,175 (8 Delta)/1,200 calls with 49 days until expiration when the market was around 1,075. The main difference between this trade and the trade you just exited the day before was not just the strikes, but that this condor was an expression of a VIX at 26 as opposed to the 19 sold previously. It's always better to sell a higher VIX than a lower one.

By February 16, the VIX drops to 22 (–15%) and the S&P is still at 1,075. You buy to close the condor for a profit of 6%. Getting out of a trade that looked weak early on and getting right back in for a more favorable VIX made the trade much easier because you took advantage of both declining volatility and time decay rather than just time decay.

Everything Goes Wrong

The Greece fear passed and the market calmed down again. Enormously. The question was, how long would market volatility stay low and the market go up? The year 2009 proved that if you wait for volatility to jump 20% every time you want to make a trade, you might not trade for a while.

This trade seemed to have everything going for it. The S&P has a 2% drop on April 16. The spike is more than a 3 standard deviation move compared to the previous 20 days. The VIX jumps 16 to almost 20, which might not seem like a lot, but it is almost a 5 standard deviation jump and price levels are touching the upper Bollinger Band. Everything looks perfect. But you do not trust the market. The VIX is still too low and you do not want to get caught with too small a condor again.

So you look for a more favorable situation. Normally you trade less than 2 and half months from expiration because you know how sensitive the condor is to jumps in volatility the farther out you go. The problem is that you can not get the premium you want for the size of condor you want to sell. Going over your checklist, the S&P is at around 1,190 to 1,200, and you want around 125 points away from the call short strike and 150 points from the put short strike, and you want at least $3 credit. The Delta for 1,050 June (63 days away) is 10 and generates a credit of about $1.50, and the 1,300 calls with 6 Delta are about $1 for a total of $2.50. That low credit is your first concern and you don't like what you see in the market. You do not want to bring the calls any lower because the market had just hit highs of 1,220 a few days before and anything less than 1,300 is too close. Remember, it is not enough that the price probably will not cross the strike price. You don't want the market to get anywhere close to your wings. Fifty points is a good maximum distance from the short strikes to tolerate.

So you do something you rarely do: sell a condor 3 months from expiration. You reason that if you sell the condor on a real spike, then a subsequent pullback in the VIX could yield a quick profit. So you sell a July 1,025/1,050, 1,325/1,350 condor for a credit of $3.30 (13%).

The market proves you correct over the next few days. You buy to close the condor within the next 2 to 3 days and make a quick 2% profit. You look at your options P&L graph and think that all you need is a few more days to nab 4%. You would have been dramatically wrong.

From an options seller's perspective, what happens next is as bad as the crash of 2008. The VIX has its largest 2-week jump in history. The VIX goes from 19 to 48 over the course of the next month, a 150% increase. The following story that plays out is graphically depicted in Figure 3.9.

SPX

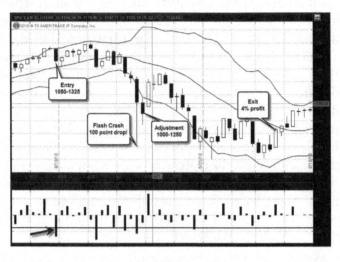

VIX

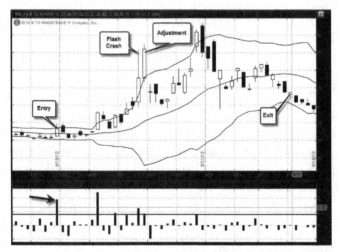

FIGURE 3.9   *Trading through the Flash Crash*

The Greece problem that had been put aside previously came back with a vengeance, and the euro started to take some serious damage. Currency prices had a real immediate impact on companies worldwide and were not something the market could ignore. There were other factors such as the government ceasing the purchase of Treasuries, an overbought market, and the complete lack of shorts. This all came to a head.

If all this wasn't bad enough, there was the infamous "Flash Crash." A market that had already fallen 40 points during the day dove almost instantly 60 points and came back all within 15 minutes. The market had hit 1,056 in about five minutes and your short strike was at 1,050. There was no adjusting, or anything else for that matter, when the market dove like that, at least not right away. The additional concern about whether to adjust right away was the actual cause of the crash. There was speculation that this was actually a computer error and everybody wanted to see how the next day would play out.

This is an actual e-mail I wrote to my clients:

> Today was an "interesting" day in the market. We closed down 38 points to 1,128. That's actually okay. Market will readjust. BUT, to make matters worse, a trader error drove the market down 100 points to 1,056. It was crazy—in the span of 15 minutes the market dropped 60 points and then came back. There was a collective gasp by traders the world over.

Even in this worst-case scenario, I wasn't worried because of two key elements about our trade: (1) we still have 70 days until expiration, and (2) we trade European-style condors, which means we really incur a loss only when we decide to take it. Nobody can force us to do anything except on expiration day. The factors of time until expiration and the type of contracts we are trading give us the time, level of security, and maneuverability to trade successfully.

Where do we go from here?

As far as I'm concerned, I see this down move as an opportunity. Down markets are actually easier to deal with than up markets. My plan is to buy to close the 1,325 contracts for a nice profit and sell them again for an additional credit at 1,250 or 1,275. I can also use some of the credit to pay to move the 1,050 down to 1,025. With the volatility so high in this trade, when things calm down we could be substantially ahead quicker than you think. Those who have been with me through the bumpy times know that I used to do this kind of thing all the time with great success.

The sole reason you could ride out this terrible roller coaster ride was because you stuck to your rules when you got into the trade. To get the $3 or 12% credit you were looking for would have required you to pull in your condor much closer on both sides. Focusing on the credit of the trade in combination with the minimum size you were looking for saved you from a killer of a trade. Imagine putting in a 4- or 5-week condor on such low volatility. You could have been wiped out.

The next day was a Friday, and toward the close the S&P was hovering at 1,100, 50 points from your short puts at 1,050, with 70 days left until expiration. Fifty points is usually as close as you like to get to your wing regardless of how much time there is until expiration. But it is a judgment call. The market could bounce the next day or keep going down. Additionally, you are going into the weekend, and you have a strong feeling that some government intervention on behalf of the euro could create a strong rally.

What do you really know about the future? Absolutely nothing. As always, all you could do is trade what was right in front of you. The perceived potential collapse of a currency is a systemic problem, and another big leg down in the market seems completely possible first thing Monday morning.

Shortly before the close when the market is at its worst and option prices are at their highest, you decide that you have to make your adjustments. Your hopes for a quick reversal that day are dashed. Capital preservation takes precedence over everything. Sure, the market could turn around on Monday, but Delta on the 1,050 is already in the upper 20s, and with every point Gamma, as depicted in Figure 3.10, showed that the losses would accumulate extremely quickly. Additionally, increasing volatility accompanying a falling market would pull the P&L curves down further and make the losses worse than the theoretical model.

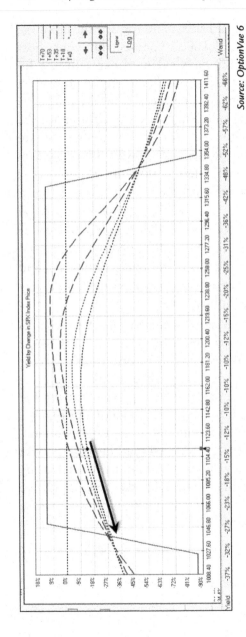

FIGURE 3.10   Gamma slide

Source: OptionVue 6

Another ugly fact is also staring you in the face. Your 1,325/1,350 calls were nearly worthless. Obviously, the value of a spread can rise higher than it can fall since value can fall only to 0. When a spread is below 50 cents and you still have a few weeks left until expiration, the spread's effectiveness as a hedge diminishes dramatically. The inability to be a good hedge is a result of two reasons. The first is the limitations of the price hedge itself because any increase in one spread greater than 50 cents is unhedged and the condor is essentially a directional trade from that point on, which was the case here. The second reason is the Delta. When Delta falls below 5, further moves away from the 5 Delta will have rapidly diminishing hedging effects. The less value there is in the call spread, the greater the damage to your position if there is a strong move in the other direction as the put spread gains value unhedged by the call spread.

Repositioning the condor so price is more centered in the condor, you buy to close the 1,325/1,350 call spread and sell the lower 1,250/1,275 spread for a credit of $2.10. Using credit garnered from lowering the call position, you buy to close the 1,025/1,050 put spread and simultaneously sell the 975/1,000 put spread for a debit of $2. Figure 3.11 shows what the adjustment does for your position.

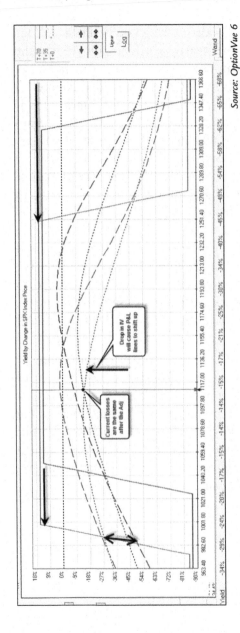

FIGURE 3.11   *Adjusting the condor*

Now with the new spreads the whole condor is shifted over, as is the risk. Essentially, you buy yourself 50 more points or another 5% move in the market. This is *after* a drop from the high of 1,220 to 1,100, which is already a 10% move down. So the market would have to experience a 20% drop from high to low in order to hit your short strike. Not that a drop that size couldn't happen, but if it did you could go through the whole process again and shift the condor by buying to close the call spread, selling a lower one and then doing the same for the put spread.

Vega is the big risk trading a condor 90 days out. You are too far away to accumulate any meaningful time decay to combat the effect of rising volatility on the condor when the drop happens. On the other hand, if the market starts to calm down and the volatility drops, the prices of the puts would also drop rapidly and the P&L curve would start to move up favorably. Regardless, you are going to be in this trade for a good while longer even if the volatility dropped because of the unrealized loss of –15%. On the other hand, if you elect to buy to close the condor you will lock in the loss of close to –15%. Before the condor could even get back to break-even, time decay and/or volatility have to eat through the loss first, which takes time.

This is the e-mail I wrote to my clients after I made my adjustments in this trade:

> I just wanted to write a quick e-mail to comfort you guys before the weekend. I moved the 1,325 to 1,250 and used the money I made from that to pay to move 1,050 to 1,000. This ends up like being in a new condor so we'll be in this for a while.

If it falls too far again, I'll just shift it over again.

If the market were to rise for some reason next week, volatility would drop, which would help our position, and I made sure that our upper side is still higher than the high for the year. If the market goes to 1,000, that would take us back to August prices in the market, which is a pretty big drop. We already dropped 10% in about a week. I think we're good to go.

My gut tells me that on Monday the market will go up and that our 1,050 would have been okay. But I only trade what is in front of me not what I think will happen.

By the way, I was completely right about the Monday opening. Over the next 3 days, the market rallied to 1173. If I had stayed in, I would have been out for a profit and that would have been it. But if the market had gone down instead of up, how could I have explained my failure to make an adjustment when I had the chance?

The expense of the Gamma slide would make the adjustment exponentially higher, requiring you to bring the calls in even closer or using some or all of your initial credit (if not more) to make the adjustment to save the principal. All of this would have required staying in the position probably as close to expiration as possible.

Markets continued to make large movements over the next month, but volatility started to drop. The S&P eventually hit a low of 1,040, but by then the time decay was eating away at the value of the condor, and the unrealized loss when you hit the low was even less than previous unrealized losses. Eventually, a rally and a drop in volatility conspired, and after 7 weeks you get out with a profit of close to 4%. For me, this trade was an example of one of the longest exposure periods to the market for one stretch, and it was during a pretty difficult time. Had you stayed in this trade, it would eventually have made even more money.

Let's review what made this trade work:

- Making sure that the condor was large

- Trading at quarter strikes

- Selling 10 Delta

- Making sure that the initial credit was high

- Making the proper adjustments to the condor to protect principal

Most of these factors are the entry rules spelled out in the preceding chapter. Some people might say that the VIX was too low and the trade should never have been initiated. The assumption with this criticism is that volatility would inevitably spike higher in the near term. Volatility can go lower and lower for a long time and many opportunities would be missed. The only thing to have done differently would have been to take the quick profit since the expiration day was so far away and the trade was still too sensitive to Vega risk. Still, hindsight always makes for an easy trade.

Ugly Trade—Crash of 2008

Many traders back-test strategies using rules that are put in place and then see what the results would be year after year. Entries and exits are somewhat subjective since volatility is defined by the subjectivity of fear; this makes back testing difficult to quantify for these condor trades. Guidelines have been offered for what a condor should look like, when it should be sold, when to adjust, and conditions for taking a profit. Every trader will have different profit objectives and risk tolerance, which will color the results of the trade.

Since everybody wants to know what a worst-case scenario would look like, the following hypothetical starts with an entry point on what was probably the worst day to make a trade. What makes this the worst trade is the huge jump in the VIX and drop in the SPX the following trading day. Ignoring all news, resistance and support, and other charts, just remember to trade the math.[1] This trade shows how to maneuver a condor through one of the most difficult markets in recent history.

During the period from September 26, 2008, to the expiration day of November 21, 2008, the market experienced incredible gyrations. The SPX moved from 1,200 down to 750, a –37% drop. The VIX surged from 32 to a high of 96, a 300% increase.

On September 26, 2008, the S&P was up 5 points to 1,214. Use one rule: Sell the November contracts closest to the quarter strike with the short strikes at 10 Delta. Figure 3.12 shows selling the November 1,375/

---

1. *Also ignore slippage in bid-ask spread and just assume execution at the midpoint price. Also ignore all transaction costs because those vary.*

1,400 calls and the 975/1,000 puts. The condor would be 375 from wing to wing. This trade produces a credit of 16.4%, nice credit and a nice size condor with 56 days until expiration. Most elements are within preferred guidelines for entering a trade. What makes this a less-than-optimum trade is that you did not take advantage of any rise in the VIX upon entering the trade.

Options	NOV <56>					
1550 calls	MktPr	MIV	Trade	Ex Pos	Delta	OrigPr
1525 calls	..$..					.....
1500 calls	1.00	26.5%			0.59	
1475 calls	0.65	23.1%			1.25	.....
1450 calls	1.15	23.3%			2.41	.....
1425 calls	1.60	22.7%			4.26	.....
1400 calls	3.70	24.6%		+4	6.96	3.70
1375 calls	6.00	25.1%		-4	10.6	6.00
1350 calls	9.60	26.0%			15.3	.....
1025 puts	10.00	37.2%			-11.2	
1000 puts	7.90	38.4%		-4	-8.80	7.90
975 puts	6.10	39.6%		+4	-6.89	6.10
950 puts	4.90	41.1%			-5.36	
925 puts	3.60	42.0%			-4.15	.....
900 puts	2.95	43.6%			-3.19	.....
875 puts	2.00	44.0%			-2.44	.....
850 puts	1.50	45.2%			-1.85	.....

Source: OptionVue 6

FIGURE 3.12   *Worst possible entry for 2008*

Monday comes and you wish you had waited for a nice down day to get in. The SPX closes down 91 points (–7.5%) to 1,122. VIX pops up 12 points (+35%) to 45, not a good way to start the week or the trade.

The first big test happens 2 weeks into the trade on October 6, 2008, when the market has another extraordinarily volatile day and moves 90 points down from high to low of the day and closes down 40 points to

1,060. Considering the speed of these drops, you decide 60 points is not enough and that this is the time to adjust the condor down.

Some timing issues when placing a trade should be examined at this point. There are two ways to look at this particular daily move. One way is that the market did a sharp reversal and the price was 60 points away from your short strike. In that case, the best strategy is to do nothing and wait. On the other hand, you could look at the day's move and consider the implication that the intraday market was within 10 points of your short strike and it is time to make an adjustment. The first way is a bit of a gamble and the latter is the more conservative approach.

When prices are falling quickly, buying to close puts is like catching a falling knife. It can be done, but it is going to hurt. The best time to adjust the put spread is when the market rallies. Even in a down market you can have huge intraday rallies. Use these rallies as opportunities to make your adjustments.

The proper way to place an order to adjust a condor requires you to turn fear and greed on its head. Greed says "don't adjust" and fear says "it's not so bad." Even if you're not watching all the horrible news, a 90-point drop should encourage you to be greedy to protect your principal and fearful of another reversal.

When the market starts to rally from its lows, using that last half-hour to make the adjustment would be optimal. The SPX closes 15 minutes after the regular market so you can keep on trading.

With the continuing fall of the market to 1,060, the 1,375/1,400 call spread that you sold for $2.30 (9%) credit is nearly worthless. Buying to close the worthless spread and selling a new spread creates a new credit. Selling the 1,225/1,250 spread generates an additional $3 (12%) in credit. Why so much? Because high volatility affects the prices of everything. Why sell the 1,225/1,250? The Delta on the 1,225 of 13 is a bit higher than Delta 10, but in a directional market you might consider taking a bit more risk in the other direction. With the extra $3 credit you are going to try to use that money to move the put spread down as much as possible. According to these numbers, you buy to close the put spread for about $6.50 and sell the 925/900 for about $4.25, the difference costing you about $2.25 and keeping about $0.75 in credit (see Figure 3.13).[2] Achieving these prices is only possible because you are making these trades into a very strong rally. Momentarily, the risk starts to increase to the calls and reduce on the puts. The new midpoint on this condor is 1,075, which isn't too bad when the market closes at 1,060. You have 135 points on the put side and 150 points on the call side with 46 days until expiration.

Two days later, the market looks as though it is capitulating when it closed at 984 after hitting a low of 970. That is a 90-point drop in 2 days. Time again to get defensive. A big flashing red light should come up whenever the market gets closer than 50 points from your short strike. The Delta on your 925 was 37. Anything over 30 and you need to consider making some adjustments (see Figure 3.14).

---

2. *It does look as though the 875/900 would produce the same result but I don't believe it.*

Options	NOV <46>					
	MktPr	MIV	Trade	Ex.Pos	Delta	OrigPr
1450 calls						
1425 calls	0.61	37.9%			0.42	.....
1400 calls	0.47	34.9%	-4	+4	0.76	3.70
1375 calls	0.40	32.4%	+4	-4	1.31	6.00
1350 calls	0.98	34.5%			2.15	.....
1325 calls	1.49	34.6%			3.37	.....
1300 calls	2.25	34.8%			5.06	.....
1275 calls	3.10	34.3%			7.31	.....
1250 calls	6.25	37.3%	+4		10.2	.....
1225 calls	9.43	38.4%	-4		13.7	.....
1025 puts	50.47	41.2%			-41.9	.....
1000 puts	42.29	43.3%	+4	-4	-36.2	7.90
975 puts	35.76	45.7%	-4	+4	-30.9	6.10
950 puts	29.21	47.1%			-26.2	.....
925 puts	24.05	49.0%	-4		-21.9	.....
900 puts	19.80	50.9%	+4		-18.2	.....
875 puts	15.71	52.1%			-14.9	.....

Source: OptionVue 6

FIGURE 3.13   *2008 crash: first adjustment*

Two days later, the market is still in full free fall. The SPX closes at 902 after hitting a low of 840. However, the S&P rises 60 points from 3 P.M. to 3:30 P.M. During that time the value of the condor is very near to break-even. Intraday moves can have tremendous effects on the price of options, and you have to be ready to take advantage of these situations in fast-moving markets. In this kind of market, you should have a limit order in place to get out at break-even or at an acceptable loss just in case you get lucky. At this point, even for a small loss it would be worth getting out of this trade and waiting for the market to calm down before putting in another one.

Options	NOV ‹44›					
1300 calls	MktPr	MIV	Trade	Ex.Pos	Delta	OrigPr
1275 calls	2.13	40.3%			2.24	.....
1250 calls	3.38	41.4%	-4	+4	3.64	6.25
1225 calls	4.37	40.7%	+4	-4	5.61	9.43
1200 calls	6.42	41.5%			8.24	.....
1175 calls	8.65	41.4%	+4		11.6	.....
1150 calls	13.17	43.4%	-4		15.7	.....
1125 calls	17.57	43.8%			20.4	.....
1100 calls	24.86	45.9%			25.8	
950 puts	55.29	54.4%			-37.7	.....
925 puts	46.36	55.8%	+4	-4	-32.2	24.05
900 puts	38.84	57.4%	-4	+4	-27.3	19.80
875 puts	32.38	59.1%			-22.9	.....
850 puts	26.68	60.5%			-18.9	.....
825 puts	21.07	61.2%	-4		-15.5	.....
800 puts	17.31	63.2%	+4		-12.6	.....
775 puts	13.90	64.7%			-10.2	.....

Source: OptionVue 6

FIGURE 3.14   *2008 crash: second adjustment*

Let's say you missed the opportunity to exit the trade, which does happen. The 825 has a Delta 31 after being in the high 40s. Another defensive move is called for. Rolling down the call spread to 1,100/1,125 where the Delta is 11 gives you a new credit of $6. There is an unusual opportunity to buy to close the put spread for under $6, leaving you only the call side to concern yourself. Of course, if you are to close the put spread then you are essentially trading directionally. The problem at this point is that a market rally could happen and then you wouldn't be hedged from the puts losing value from the accompanying drop in volatility. So you decide to buy to close the put spread and sell the strike under 10

Delta, which will be a 625/650. So with the market sitting at 900, you have a condor extending from 650 to 1,100, or 550 points with only 42 days remaining (see Figure 3.15).

Options	NOV <42>					
1225 calls	MktPr	MIV	Trade	Ex Pos	Delta	OrigPr
1200 calls	3.49	52.6%			3.30	.....
1175 calls	5.31	54.4%	-4	+4	4.71	8.65
1150 calls	5.95	52.6%	+4	-4	6.55	13.17
1125 calls	8.67	54.2%	+4		8.87	.....
1100 calls	13.71	58.1%	-4		11.7	.....
1075 calls	15.36	56.0%			15.1	.....
1050 calls	22.50	59.8%			19.1	.....
825 puts	47.14	64.5%	+4	-4	-32.3	21.07
800 puts	41.86	68.8%	-4	+4	-27.5	17.31
775 puts	32.81	68.3%			-23.3	.....
750 puts	28.90	72.3%			-19.5	.....
725 puts	21.84	71.7%			-16.1	.....
700 puts	19.05	75.5%			-13.2	.....
675 puts	14.81	76.4%			-10.8	.....
650 puts	12.12	79.0%	-4		-8.68	.....
625 puts	9.10	79.7%	+4		-6.94	.....

Source: OptionVue 6

FIGURE 3.15   *2008 crash: third adjustment*

Every time you bought to close calls, you bought them for less than you paid for them, so there was actually a credit that you got to keep. After this adjustment, you have accumulated a credit worth 28% of your margin. Now it is just a matter of waiting to break even or making a profit. Figure 3.16 shows what this final condor looks like.

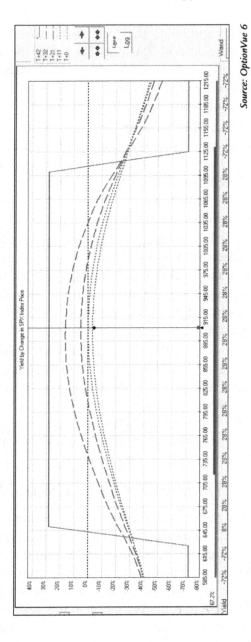

FIGURE 3.16 *2008 crash: final condor*

Source: OptionVue 6

By expiration, the SPX barely breaks 1,000 and reaches a low of 750 (the day before expiration), both well within your range. So this would have been a winning trade at the end of the day. This is not to say you should stay until expiration but the adjustments did work.

In all likelihood, trading through this horrific time would have been much more difficult than presented here. The bid-ask spread probably would have made each adjustment more expensive. Nonetheless, the process, reasoning, and approach are legitimate and very well could have been executed.

The key to successful adjustments is to be nimble and decisive. Know why you are making an adjustment. When the market is moving against you, the only consideration for doing any adjustment should be preservation of capital and not profit. If you guard the condor ferociously, profits will most likely result.

If you are still in the trade the week before expiration, you should look for an exit point even at a loss. During options expiration week, the market starts off making large moves and settles down at the end of the week. There is no telling which way the market will jump, and it can just as easily move against you as for you.

Trading an Out-of-Control Rally

Many traders lose money in bear-market rallies because the rally apparently seems irrational. This sentiment feeds itself. Traders who were betting the market would keep going down found themselves buying the market in order to stop their losses as the market went up. The more people who are bearish at any one time, the faster the market will go up in a frenzy of buying.

In the environment of disbelief, condor sellers initially bask in the sun of declining volatility only to have it snatched away by higher Delta and higher Gamma. No trade is a sure thing. The following illustrates the follies of overconfidence and disbelief.

From July to August of 2009, the market moves from 900 to 1,005 in a trend straight up, which may not seem like a lot but is a 11.6% jump in a very fidgety environment. The drop in volatility makes traders reluctant to make what could potentially be a disastrous adjustment. A sharp reversal would not only bring you much closer to your puts, but it would also be accompanied by a higher volatility resulting in a double whammy against you in higher prices. Here is a hypothetical trade entered at the worst possible time.

On July 10, 2009, the SPX closes at 879. You place the trade just under the Delta 10 to generate a credit of $3 or 12% on margin. Right away, one red flag with this trade is that there is not enough time until expiration, nor is it large enough. When trading in a market with a strong up trend, try to sell when the VIX has some sort of spike.

The trade was August 750/755 puts and 975/1,000 calls with 42 days until expiration, for a 15% credit.

The SPX is up to 934 on July 16. The accompanying drop in volatility exposes the difficulty in adjusting this condor. This position is down 9% and the Delta is at 27. Figure 3.17 shows how difficult it is to roll up the calls. If you roll the puts up a full 50 points, you garner only $2.30 in credit, while it costs $3.90 to roll up the calls 25 points for a net debit of $1.60.

What is particularly nerve-racking is that the put side is a mere 100 points away from the current price, which would be vulnerable to a sharp reversal. The market continues to go straight up to 1,000 over the next 3 weeks, which means that this trade requires at least one more adjustment. This was the "no way" trade because all the prognosticators were saying "no way" could the market continue to go up in this manner. You wanted to believe all these "experts" but it didn't help; they were wrong. You always have to trade what is in front of you. The main lesson to learn from this example is while a shrinking volatility can benefit condor trades, a sharp up move means you might have to fight Gamma. In order to collect the credit necessary to roll up the call side, you will have to bring the put side uncomfortably close. Regardless, do what you have to do and trade the math.

Options	AUG <37>					
1125 calls	MktPr	MIV	Trade	Ex.Pos	Delta	OrigPr
1100 calls	0.15	21.8%			0.29	.....
1075 calls	0.55	22.5%			1.15	.....
1050 calls	0.70	20.2%			3.42	.....
1025 calls	1.70	20.3%	+4		8.11	.....
1000 calls	4.10	20.6%	-8	+4	16.0	0.95
975 calls	9.70	22.1%	+4	-4	27.0	2.30
950 calls	18.30	23.3%			40.1	.....
925 calls>	30.90	24.7%			53.5	.....
875 puts	11.50	27.3%			-24.7	.....
850 puts	7.50	29.1%			-17.4	.....
825 puts	5.10	31.5%	-4		-12.0	.....
800 puts	3.30	33.2%	+4		-8.24	.....
775 puts	2.20	35.5%	+4	-4	-5.64	6.80
750 puts	1.75	38.7%	-4	+4	-3.85	4.40
725 puts	1.00	39.9%			-2.64	.....
700 puts	0.75	42.5%			-1.81	.....

Source: OptionVue 6

FIGURE 3.17   *Out of control rally: condor adjustment*

The trades in the month of July were quite different. In Figure 3.18, you see how two quick actual trades were executed while yielding good returns. When you see the market rally, you choose to wait until it looks as though the rally is over before selling options. At the end of June, there is a down day with a jump in the VIX and you sell a condor. Within a few days you are able to take your profits. Then you wait more than 2 weeks before putting in another trade. If you had chosen to remain in the first position to try to make more profits, you would have quickly regretted it because the market kept going up. Exposure to market risk is not worth the risk that it can move against you. Just take the money and wait for the next opportunity. There is always a next opportunity.

Source: thinkorswim by TD Ameritrade

FIGURE 3.18   *Two short profitable trades*

A quick review of some adjustment rules:

- It is easier to adjust in a down market because you get more for rolling down the call credit spreads.

- It is harder to adjust in an up market because you don't get much for rolling up the put credit spread and you bring the position closer to your downside risk.

- Trade the math: Don't let Deltas go over 25 to 30.

- When possible, adjust when the market is moving in the opposite direction intraday. Adjust the puts when the market rallies or adjust the calls when the market dips.

- Trade only what is in front of you and not what you or anybody else thinks the market will do.

- If you must speculate, assume the worst-case, not the best-case, scenario.

- If you must adjust, consider getting out at break-even at the first chance available.

- You can always put in a new trade with better strikes.

Risk Management

Other strategies may reduce your exposure to risk. The adjustment strategy is only one facet of risk management. The goal has been to minimize exposure to time in the market and to maximize gains.

Take the Loss

The most unpleasant risk-management strategy is taking a loss. Sometimes you will have to take a loss but that is all part of the game. If you make 4% a month for several months, you can afford to take a 5% or 10% loss if necessary. Insisting on 100% wins means you will one day push a trade too far. With the strategies outlined previously, a losing trade might not happen for years. Patiently waiting for good entry points and quick exits out of the market reduces your exposure to the market and therefore to market risk.

Reduce Your Exposure

Buying to close half or a third of a condor can derive from different motivations. One motivation is to minimize loss. So instead of taking a loss on the entire position, you take off part of the trade at a loss and keep trading the rest of the condor with less money at risk. Another reason to buy to close part of the condor is to capture a quick small profit with the intention of grabbing a larger profit by remaining in the rest of the condor for a longer period for perhaps greater profits. Of course, you'll be exposing yourself to further market risk. But have a specific target in mind regarding time to remain in the trade, the level of loss you are able to take with the rest of the condor, and how much more gain you are looking to capture as a trigger for closing the trade.

Wing Buyback

A third strategy is buying to close all or part of one side of the condor. When you're making an adjustment, the technique is to buy to close one spread and sell a more expensive spread. When making an adjustment, you want to buy to close the spread when it is worth less than what you sold it for originally so that you can capture a profit from that trade. There are three reasons a spread will lose value: decreasing volatility, time decay, and a change in market direction. When the market moves quickly in one direction, the chances are that the diminished value of the spread in the other direction will become an opportunity to buy to close and then to sell a different strike. If the reason the spread loses value is because of decreased volatility or time decay, it might be an opportunity to buy to close all or some of that side of the condor. Volatility could always rise on one hand, and on the other hand there might not be a lot left for time value to fall any further to diminish the value of that spread.

Buying to close one side of a condor makes sense only in two scenarios. The first scenario is when you have a strong conviction that the market will reverse direction so that the value of the condor falls enough to create profits. If correct, you will be able to buy to close the spread at pennies on the dollar and then sell the other spread at a higher price when the reversal occurs. Although this works, don't wait too long to close the remaining spread. If after a few days you have still not bought to close the remaining spread, if you were wrong in your timing, you still have the other side to hedge.

Trading condors can make a lot of money but only if you are very careful. There is no reward without risk. The risk in condors is always substantial and the rewards are commensurate. But through the use of the insights presented here you will have a better chance of succeeding with profitable trades.

Chapter 4

Day Trading Condors

Throughout the book, you have studied a very specific strategy, selling condors for their time value. The basics of the strategy are to sell large condors 6 to 8 weeks away from expiration and to get out a month before expiration. In that strategy you can sell condors on stocks, ETFs, or—best of all—indexes because of their lower sensitivity to news on individual companies.

There is another way to make money selling condors more akin to a day-trading strategy by selling ahead of major news events. The idea of selling condors prior to a big news event seems contradictory to everything you have learned about condors so far. Selling condors is supposed to be about time decay and stability in price. You know for a fact that before major announcements, a stock's price is *unstable* and that there is a high probability the stock will move more than usual the day after the news announcement. On the surface, this strategy seems counterintuitive. Nonetheless, all the fundamental principles of how Theta, Gamma, Delta, and Vega work are exactly the same but with aggressive dynamics. Whereas the centerpiece of condor selling has been the decay of Theta, the focus on this second type of trade is purely on volatility, or a Vega play.

A Little About Earnings

Every company announces their earnings quarterly. After the report is issued, markets can react dramatically, tepidly, or not at all. The cause of the move is at times a mystery to traders. It is not unusual for the markets to punish positive earnings reports or reward poor earnings because it all depends on "expectations." Even meeting or exceeding expectations doesn't always help. So although there might be a cause and effect from earnings reports to price action, the thread behind the market's collective reasoning is often tenuous. Regardless of the reasons involved, stock prices can act dramatically so traders of all stripes will try to find a way to take advantage of this probability and make a quick profit.

The ordinary stock trader usually just buys stock if he thinks there will be a big jump the next day. There is always the possibility to short the stock, planning to sell high and buy low, but in an IRA you are not normally allowed to go short. Even if you could short the stock, your chances are 50/50 that price action will be in your favor, no better than buying the stock. If you're wrong, at best, you'll be down a few percentage points. At worst, the stock could be in a sharp new trend in the wrong direction and you decide to wait it out for whatever reason, increasing your losses.

When trading stocks long or short, you can make money only if you get the direction right. No one can guarantee with any certainty that, on a specific date, a stock will go up or down in price. Traders guess and wager but no one knows for sure. You can say the same thing about volatility. Predicting volatility is exactly like predicting direction because implied volatility usually goes up when the stock goes down. Just because you are a volatility trader does not by itself mean you have any meaningful edge.

However, there are a few very important exceptions in which there is certainty regarding the rise and fall of volatility. One exception occurs around earnings announcements. This is one of those events written in stone, and you can count on it four times a year. Hand in hand with this certainty is the increase in implied volatility the day before earnings are announced. Everyone wants to take advantage of this certainty. The universal question is, how?

The day before earnings announcements the stock price is likely to be relatively calm. Stock price is supposed to move up on good news and down on bad news, so most traders don't want to take a big bet in one direction or the other before the big earnings news is announced. Anticipation is very high before the announcement. If the stock has a history of volatile fluctuations, this only adds to the uncertainty of the market's reaction after the earnings news.

Some options traders advocate buying at-the-money calls and puts, called a long straddle, right before the earnings announcements. On the one hand, your potential loss is limited to the price of the options, and on the other hand, the potential for gains is unlimited if the move is large enough. This rationale makes sense on its surface. You place a bet that the market will move up or down. What could go wrong?

Losing money is easier than you think. Travel back in time to a couple of weeks before the earnings announcement. Put yourself on the other side of a straddle. Imagine you are the seller of the at-the-money puts and calls. Let's say the stock XYZ is currently at $100 and you think the stock could move a maximum $10 up or down by expiration. As a seller, how much would you sell these at-the-money calls and put options for? You wouldn't sell either the put or the calls for less than $10, so you'd probably ask at least $20 for the straddle.

Examine the different outcomes for this trade. If the market moves up $10, you as the seller have to pay $10 on the calls you sold, and you keep the difference of $10 on the puts you sold. The only way you start to lose money on the trade is if the stock moves more than $20 in either direction. The straddle buyer needs one side of the trade to be 200% wrong in order to make any money. The only problem is that this trade is naked on both sides, and you are exposing yourself to more risk than a condor if the price shoots up or down substantially. Since violent moves are not uncommon after earnings announcements, you would like to increase probabilities even more in your favor.

Two weeks go by and you are up against the earnings announcement. Keep in mind that you are also 2 weeks closer to expiration. Normally, after 2 weeks of time decay these options might be worth only $16, $8 for each side of the straddle, but with all the fear associated with the earnings announcement, the price has jumped up to $20. As a seller of the straddle, you'll sell for two reasons. The first reason is that, as before, you still don't think the price will move more than $20 in either direction by expiration. The second reason is that you also know that the fear and speculation right before earnings are inflating the prices. After the earnings are announced, there will be nothing to be afraid of anymore because there will be no more uncertainty. When the fear gets sucked out of the price of the options, reflected in a drop in implied volatility, the $20 options could be worth $16 or less.

One way to increase the odds in your favor is to trade the higher volatility. Remember that higher volatility does *not* mean that the volatility number before the earnings announcement is wrong. There is no claim here that the prices are somehow overinflated. All you know with near certainty is that volatility will be lower the next day. The greater the drop in volatility, the more the drop favors the seller who sold at a high volatility, especially if the higher volatility was unfounded by reports of an uninteresting earnings announcement.

The other way to increase the odds of success is to trade the lower Delta. Compare the straddle to a condor by using an example from Apple. With Apple at $250, the at-the-money call and put for September 2010 each cost $8 for a total cost of $16 ($1,600). An Apple Condor with Deltas at 10 or lower has a range between 230 and 280. Whereas the straddle sellers and buyers are debating whether the price could move $16, the condor seller needs the price to move more than $30 in either direction to lose any money. Looking at the example shown in Figure 4.1, you can see that the straddle depicted here would earn the buyer 80% returns (with the seller obviously suffering equivalent losses) if the price moved $30 in either direction, but the condor seller would still break even.

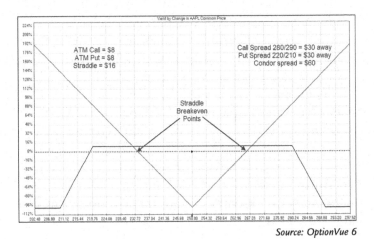

Source: OptionVue 6

FIGURE 4.1   *Straddle versus condor*

Not all earnings announcements or stocks are created equal. You may investigate the best conditions to place a trade that will take advantage of increased volatility with each company. There is risk in this trade just as in any other. In fact, there will be times you will lose big but you can mitigate the risk.

The Perfect Setup and Trade

First you want to determine how much of an edge you get from selling before earnings. The determining factor on whether to sell a condor before earnings is a skew in volatility and its subsequent collapse. When selling condors for time decay, keep an eye on implied volatility versus historical volatility. If the implied is greater than the historical, the trade favors the seller, using past behavior as an indication of future fluctuations. This skew looks into the future instead of the past.

Figure 4.2 is an example of Amazon (AMZN) the day before earnings on Thursday, April 22, 2010, the May at-the-money calls were priced at a 48.2% implied volatility. Compare that with the volatility in June with 41.4% volatility and July with 39.0% volatility.

Options	MAY <30>			JUN <58>			JUL <86>		
175 calls	MktPr	MIV	Delta	MktPr	MIV	Delta	MktPr	MIV	Delta
170 calls	1.91	45.7%	18.8	3.05	39.5%	23.8	4.20	37.2%	27.4
165 calls	2.89	46.1%	25.7	4.20	39.8%	30.2	5.50	37.6%	33.4
160 calls	4.25	46.8%	34.0	5.70	40.1%	37.4	7.10	37.9%	39.9
155 calls	6.05	47.6%	43.2	7.65	40.6%	45.3	9.10	38.5%	46.9
150 calls>	8.35	48.2%	52.9	9.95	41.4%	53.5	11.40	39.0%	53.9
145 calls	10.95	48.5%	62.6	12.65	42.1%	61.5	14.15	40.0%	60.9
140 calls	14.15	49.0%	71.8	15.70	42.8%	69.1	17.15	40.6%	67.6
135 calls	17.70		79.9	19.30	44.0%	75.9	20.60	41.7%	73.7

Source: OptionVue 6

FIGURE 4.2   *Monthly volatility skew*

In Table 4.1, you see that volatility had been rising steadily for the previous few days. Three days earlier on Monday, the implied volatility for the at-the-money-call was 42.5%. The logical conclusion for the rise in volatility would be an accompanying drop in the price of the stock, because when stocks go up, volatility goes down. Not in this case.

TABLE 4.1   *Simultaneous Rise in Price and Volatility Prior to Earnings for AMZN*

	Before		After		
	4/19/2010	4/20/2010	4/21/2010	4/22/2010	4/23/2010
Stock Price	142	144	146	150	145
Implied Volatility	42.50%	42.50%	43.70%	48.30%	30.80%

Source: OptionVue 6

Ahead of the earnings announcement, market price of the stock went up steadily the entire week. As you can see in Table 4.1, volatility also rose gradually and popped right before the earnings announcement. The day after earnings were released, volatility collapsed from 48% to 30%, or a full 37.5% drop. The stock price also dropped.

A condor trade would have been interesting on AMZN right before and after the earnings announcement. You let the Deltas be your guide. Know nothing about the company, history, or industry, just trade the math. In this trade (see Figure 4.3), you sell the 125/130 puts and the 175/180 calls. The credit is 20% of the margin at risk.

Notice also the value of a straddle at 150. The calls are worth 8.35 and the puts are 7.95. A long straddle buyer needs the market to move more than 16.30 in either direction by expiration in order to make money in the trade. The call side is $25 away and the puts are $20 away.

Actuals	AMZN Common		Legend	
	150.09	+3.66	MktPr	Chg
Options	**MAY <30>**			
195 calls	MktPr	MIV	Trade	Delta
190 calls	0.28	44.6%		2.74
185 calls	0.48	45.1%		4.65
180 calls	0.77	45.0%	+20	7.54
175 calls	1.23	45.3%	-20	11.7
170 calls	1.91	45.7%		17.3
165 calls	2.89	46.1%		24.4
160 calls	4.25	46.8%		32.9
155 calls	6.05	47.6%		42.6
150 calls>	8.35	48.3%		52.8
150 puts>	7.95	46.6%		-47.2
145 puts	5.60	47.0%		-37.1
140 puts	3.70	46.8%		-27.7
135 puts	2.42	47.5%		-19.7
130 puts	1.42	47.5%	-20	-13.2
125 puts	0.85	48.7%	+20	-8.34
120 puts	0.50	50.4%		-4.95
115 puts	0.27	51.4%		-2.74
110 puts	0.15	53.5%		-1.42

Source: OptionVue 6

FIGURE 4.3   *AMZN condor day trade*

The fundamentals of a condor are always the same. All the Greeks are still in play. Figure 4.4 is a standard condor graph. Based on the first dotted line, which represents today, any sharp moves in the market immediately register as a losing trade. The second line shows that if the price is at the same level in 16 days the value of the condor should reach 11%. This two-dimensional graph doesn't simultaneously show the third dimension of the trade, which is the effect of volatility.

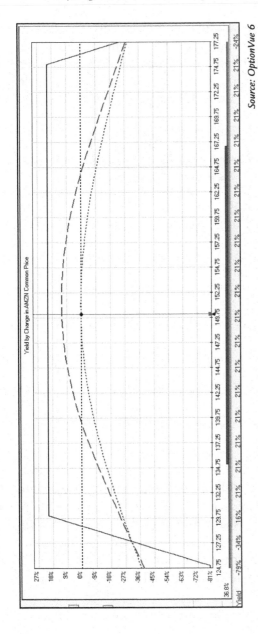

FIGURE 4.4   *AMZN condor day trade graphic P&L analysis*

Nothing conveys the importance of volatility better than the visuals in these two graphs. Within the first half hour after the open the next day, the earnings announcement had been completely digested into the price of the stock. It really doesn't matter whether earnings were good or bad. The market was unimpressed in either direction. The market did decide that uncertainty had diminished; so had the price of the options. The value of the condor plummeted and the trade yielded an 11% profit overnight as can be seen in Figure 4.5.

This trade was successful because you traded the math; you traded Vega. Although there are other pieces of information to consider before putting on the trade, any additional information will have no effect on the trade's profitability or likelihood of success. Further research helps you decide whether the trade is worth putting on or whether it should be left alone.

Most of the same conditions that guided your condor trade still apply. The first of these is price. A stock with a high price will have many different strike prices. But it is not just the number of strikes that is significant. You have to look at the Deltas and see how much they jump from one strike to the next. The Delta should vary by a few points from strike to strike. You don't want to see a Delta of 30 on one strike and 10 on the next. That kind of range doesn't give you a lot of choices. If the jump is too large, the stock is not useful. You want to see high open interest and volume in the options. The window of profitability might be very small and you want to be able to trade quickly and without losing too much on the bid-ask spread.

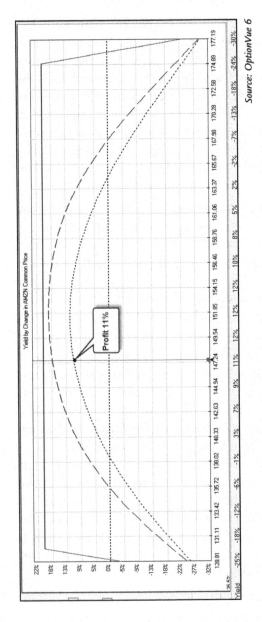

FIGURE 4.5   *AMZN condor day trade: winning trade*

Source: OptionVue 6

The Process

A review of option opportunities on Friday, July 16, 2010, expiration day showed the following: An earnings trade was 30 days away from expiration, so you could look at the other extreme, only one day from expiration. Table 4.2 shows the results of a program that looks specifically for volatility skews from one month to the next. To rank the results, the program divides the first month by the second month. If the number is over 1, there is a skew. Anything under 1 is not worth considering.

Number 1 on the list didn't surprise me. Google frequently announces earnings the night before expiration Friday. Naturally, with only one day left, IV goes through the ceiling because the market doesn't care that it is expiration Friday and will move whatever number of points it thinks is correct. The option pricing has to accommodate the projected range for a one-day move after an earnings report from a heavily traded stock.

At the end of Thursday, everybody who was buying and selling options about to expire was speculating. If a trader really wanted to hedge their Google position, it would be far cheaper to buy next month's puts with implied volatility of 32% than to pay 79% for one day's worth of protection. Because this trade is so speculative, volatility is high, almost two-and-a-half times higher than the next month.

Figure 4.6 gives you a look into the past to see how much Google tends to move on expiration day.

TABLE 4.2   *Volatility Skew Candidates for Day Trade*

	Asset Name	Symbol	Sort Value	IV.1stMo	IV.2ndMo	IV.3rdMo	Avg. Tot. $Volume (5)	Underly Last
1	Google	GOOG	2.45	79.2	32.3	30.5	56,274	494.02
2	Goldman Sachs Group	GS	1.50	56.7	37.8	35.3	19,532	145.22
3	BP Prudhoe Bay Trust	BPT	1.09	26.8	24.7	29.9	4,125	91.37
4	Potash Saskatchewan	POT	1.06	41.2	38.9	38.2	6,999	98.49
5	PNC Financial Services	PNC	1.05	37.0	35.3	37.0	1,182	60.88
6	Diamonds Trust Series	DIA	0.97	19.5	20.2	20.7	4,650	103.70

Source: OptionVue 6

Date / Time (ET)	Announcement	Same Day [if bmo]		Next Day [if amc]	
		gap	close	gap	close
15 Jul 10 amc	Q2 2010 Google	0.08	0.55	.	.
15 Apr 10 amc	Q1 2010 Google	0.54	1.07	-5.43	-7.59
21 Jan 10 amc	Q4 2009 Google	0.52	0.44	-3.17	-5.66
15 Oct 09 amc	Q3 2009 Google	-0.29	-1.01	3.29	3.76
16 Jul 09	Q2 2009 Google	-0.34	1.01	-2.17	-2.79
16 Apr 09 amc	Q1 2009 Google	0.53	2.43	-0.70	0.90
22 Jan 09 amc	Q4 2008 Google	-1.66	1.13	0.90	5.94
16 Oct 08	Q3 2008 Google	-1.89	4.08	7.35	5.53
17 Jul 08 amc	Q2 2008 Google	-0.27	-0.40	-6.58	-9.77
17 Apr 08 amc	Q1 2008 Google	0.28	-1.06	19.06	19.99
31 Jan 08 amc	Q4 2007 Google	-1.69	2.92	-6.31	-8.58
18 Oct 07 amc	Q3 2007 Google	0.30	0.97	2.35	0.80

Skews of Implied Volatility

IV1	IV2	IV3
79.20%	32.30%	30.50%
Skew IV2 to IV1 46.90%	Skew IV3 to IV2 1.80%	

Source: DiscoverOptions

FIGURE 4.6   *GOOG earnings moves*

The column on the right shows the percentage move from one day to the next when earnings were announced. There have been some pretty serious price jumps. No matter how far apart your spread was on April 17, 2008, you got blown out the next day, when Google was up 90 points, or +19%. These types of 20% moves demonstrate the risk inherent in trading individual stocks rather than indexes. Sometimes you lose, which is why you are wise to keep the amount of risk small.

Ignoring those once-in-a-blue-moon spectacular price leaps, you shouldn't be dissuaded by large moves by themselves. What matters is not the size of the move in percentage terms but how well the market priced condors at the low Deltas. In other words, did it still turn out profitably even after a hefty 7.5% move? Could you still execute your trade and make money or break even because of the high volatility?

The guideline for a trade is to seek Deltas below 10 for the short strike. On the call side you might choose to be more aggressive because the bigger moves, with one notable exception in this case, are usually down. The goal is to see how this trade would have fared the next day. With the IV at 72% (two-and-a-half times the next month's IV) you would have sold the 540/550 puts and the 650/660 calls for a credit worth 8.5% on your margin with Google at $595 (see Figure 4.7). Google closed at $550 right at the lower strike. So that trade would have cost you nothing except commission. On to the next trade, right?

You are a trader, remember. These "day trading" condors have to be watched and traded waiting for just the right opportunity. Just because the price closed at $550 doesn't mean the position was worthless from the open.

In fact, right at the open Google was at $565 and the position was worth 7.2% (see Figure 4.8). An hour later it was worth almost the whole 8%. As the day moved and the stock continued dropping, it stayed profitable but less so until 3 P.M. At 3:30 it started to lose money as the price moved to $555, only 5 points away from the short strike with 30 minutes left to go.

Actuals	GOOG Common		Legend	
	595.30	+6.30	MktPr	Chg
Options	APR <2>			
680 calls	MktPr	MIV	Trade	Delta
670 calls	0.35	80.3%		2.53
660 calls	0.80	84.2%		4.09
650 calls	0.90	76.2%	+10	6.52
640 calls	1.30	71.8%	-10	10.2
630 calls	2.35	71.4%		15.6
620 calls	4.00	70.9%		23.0
610 calls	6.40	70.0%		32.8
600 calls>	10.50	72.1%		44.8
600 puts>	14.70	69.3%		-55.2
590 puts	9.20	66.8%		-42.0
580 puts	5.50	66.7%		-29.5
570 puts	2.95	66.3%		-19.2
560 puts	1.55	67.9%		-11.5
550 puts	0.90	71.1%	-10	-6.29
540 puts	0.40	72.0%	+10	-3.17
530 puts	0.25	76.1%		-1.46
520 puts	0.10			-0.61

Source: OptionVue 6

FIGURE 4.7   *GOOG day trade*

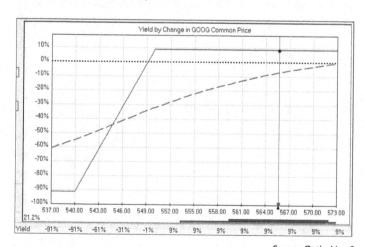

Source: OptionVue 6

FIGURE 4.8   *GOOG at the open*

The main lesson here is that the "trade ain't over till it's over." The smart move after hearing the bad news was to just take the money at the open and call it a day. For a quick trade it did pretty well, considering how bad a day it was.

Now look at the Google trade in front of you. You already know that the IV is predictably high. Don't look at the charts just to see where you are.

Looking at Figure 4.9, you see that Google had quite a rally from a low in the $440s to almost $500 in 2 weeks. It also looks as though it was reaching a previous high, which can serve as a warning flag. Still, the price could continue going up. It sure looked as though the market had already priced a great deal of good news into the trade.

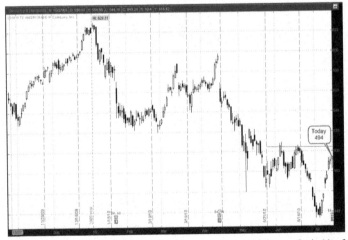

Source: OptionVue 6

FIGURE 4.9   *GOOG price graph*

With these day trades, being a brilliant technical analyst doesn't help much because the earnings news will create a temporary blip in the trade anyway, which charting doesn't predict. Still, just looking at this, it is likely that either a slight rise, a small profit-taking move, or a big drop would happen. So you need to be worried about downside risk.

This is the story the options market is telling you. Looking at the price of the at-the-money calls, the sellers think the price will go up $13.50 at the most. Interestingly, the at-the-money-puts are only $9.80 even with such a high volatility, clearly showing a bias to the upside.

Looking at Figure 4.10, if you decide to sell the 530/540 with a Delta of 10, you get $0.55 credit. If you go up one strike, to the 540/550, you also get the same credit. Notice that the IV on $540 is higher than that on $550 or $530. These price distortions happen sometimes depending on the demand for certain strikes. Therefore, it makes sense to take the high spread with less risk. On the put side don't even ask yourself the question; just go as low as you can and still make money, which is 450/440. The total credit is worth 9.8%. You could go lower but there just isn't any money in it.

Options	JUL ‹2›						
580 calls	MktPr	MIV	Trade	Ex Pos	Delta	OrigPr	
570 calls	0.30	95.4%			0.78	......	
560 calls	0.35	88.7%			1.60	......	
550 calls	0.40	79.8%	+10		3.16	......	
540 calls	0.95	80.7%	-10		5.96	......	
530 calls	1.50	76.3%			10.7	......	
520 calls	2.75	75.5%			18.0	......	
510 calls	5.50	79.7%			28.5	......	
500 calls	8.50	77.0%			42.0	......	
490 calls›	13.50	78.0%			57.2	......	
490 puts›	9.80	80.5%			-42.8	......	
480 puts	6.20	83.0%			-28.7	......	
470 puts	3.30	81.3%			-17.5	......	
460 puts	1.75	82.9%			-9.70	......	
450 puts	0.90	85.1%	-10		-4.90	......	
440 puts	0.40	85.8%	+10		-2.25	......	
430 puts	0.25	92.5%			-0.95	......	
420 puts	0.15				-0.37	......	
410 puts	0.05				-0.13	......	
400 puts	0.05				-0.04	......	

Source: OptionVue 6

FIGURE 4.10   *GOOG day trade 2*

Next Morning

The news was bad. Google was taking a big hit and opened down 25 points to $469, a 5% move. In this situation, you should get out right away. Sure, you have another 19 points but who knows how far down this could go? You get 9% by getting out right away. It's not worth staying in for even another minute. Figure 4.11 shows what the screenshot looked like in the first minute.

So what happened at the end of the day? Does it even matter? After your trade is done, so is your interest.

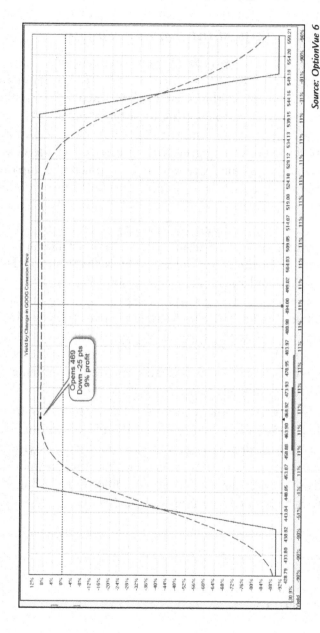

FIGURE 4.11 *GOOG day trade at the open*

Source: OptionVue 6

Important Announcements

There is one more type of event that can have a deep impact on volatility: Any kind of government announcement. Perhaps the FDA is scheduled to make a decision about a new drug for a pharmaceutical company. Maybe an important ruling on a court case or an expected vote in Congress will directly affect the company. Any planned event that can affect a company when the outcome is not predictable will cause volatility to rise.

At the end of the trading day (exactly 3:27 P.M. according to the pop in the charts), another nice opportunity also came up the day before expiration. The Securities and Exchange Commission (SEC) announced that they were going to make a "Significant Announcement" about Goldman Sachs (GS) at 4:45 P.M., right after the close of the market. In 33 minutes GS rose from $140 to $145, a 3.5% move. The buzz was that the SEC and GS had negotiated a settlement, and that rumor made the stock price rally.

In one hour, the volatility went straight up from 30% to 56% (see Figure 4.12). By all indications, the market had already priced in the good news. A rise in volatility defies normal reasoning because the market was soaring at the same time. Straddles were selling for about $5 (calls $2.48 and puts $2.35).

GS 3 P.M. ET

Options	JUL <2>		
160 calls	MktPr	MIV	Delta
155 calls	0.03		0.07
150 calls	0.06		1.19
145 calls	0.24	33.5%	13.7
140 calls>	1.89	30.4%	64.3
135 calls	6.20		98.8
130 calls	11.15		100
155 puts	13.90		-100
150 puts	8.95		-98.8
145 puts	4.15		-86.3
140 puts>	0.77	30.1%	-35.7
135 puts	0.09		-1.21
130 puts	0.03		0.00
125 puts	0.03		0.00

GS 4 P.M. ET

Options	JUL <2>		
160 calls	MktPr	MIV	Delta
155 calls	0.40	70.5%	11.3
150 calls	1.06	64.9%	25.2
145 calls>	2.48	55.2%	52.3
140 calls	5.80		80.2
135 calls	10.40		94.0
130 calls	15.25		98.6
155 puts	10.35		-88.7
150 puts	5.85		-74.8
145 puts>	2.38	58.2%	-47.7
140 puts	0.73	60.1%	-19.8
135 puts	0.23	67.9%	-6.00
130 puts	0.08		-1.42
125 puts	0.04		-0.28

Source: OptionVue 6

FIGURE 4.12   *GS announcement*

The problem with this trade was the credit you could have gotten for putting on a condor. A 10 Delta condor garnered only a 5% credit on margin (see Figure 4.13). That seemed like a lot of risk for such a small possible return. The Deltas also took very large jumps because there were relatively fewer strikes.

By all indications, the good news could have had a further upside effect. The likelihood was that any good news was probably priced in, limiting further upside moves. Another 10-point move was 6.8% on top of the 3.5% that had already occurred.

Actuals	GS Common		Legend	
	145.22	+6.16	MktPr	Chg
Options	JUL <2>			
165 calls	MktPr	MIV	Trade	Delta
160 calls	0.26	85.7%	+20	5.17
155 calls	0.40	70.5%	-20	11.3
150 calls	1.06	64.9%		25.2
145 calls>	2.48	55.2%		52.3
140 calls	5.80			80.2
135 calls	10.40			94.0
155 puts	10.35			-88.7
150 puts	5.85			-74.8
145 puts>	2.38	58.2%		-47.7
140 puts	0.73	60.1%		-19.8
135 puts	0.23	67.9%	-20	-6.00
130 puts	0.08		+20	-1.42
125 puts	0.04			-0.28

Source: OptionVue 6

FIGURE 4.13   *GS day trade*

The next day, GS opened up 6 points but never managed to stay over $150. An hour into the trading day the
condor was nearly worthless. So even in a less-than-
perfect situation the trade worked.

Day trading by definition is a very risky trade. The
leverage effect of options only amplifies the risk dimension. The objectives here as in the previous trades are to
use the pieces of information the option prices give you
to set up a trade. The changes in volatility provide
opportunities for entry and exit. Deltas tell you what
the market thinks is an outside chance for price to reach
a certain level. By eliminating opinion and conjecture
and just looking at what the option prices themselves
are telling you through the Greeks, you should greatly
increase your chances for profit and success.

I N D E X

A

acceleration, 25
   options trading, 24
adjustment rules, 147
adjustments, sideways markets, 112-115, 118
Amazon, earnings announcements, 157-161
American-style options, 50-51
Apple, 40
assignment, 50
Augen, Jeff, 72

B

Baruch, Bernard, 8
Beta, 52
Bollinger Bands, 73-74
bonus features, 49
buy-and-hold strategy, 9
buyers, 16-18

C

call short strikes, 90
change in price, 25

charts, selling condors, position, 71-75
comparing condors, 64
ConAgra, 42
condor strategies, 62
condors, 5-8
   comparing, 64
   researching, 40-46, 49
   selling, 62
      position, 68-69
      position, charts, 71-75
      position, Delta, 75-80
      position, fundamentals, 69-71
      price, 80-82
      time, 63-68
   time decay, 61
   trading, 84-85
      reasons for, 85-89
   versus straddles, 156
contrarians, 22
counterintuitive, 22
crash of 2008, 136-144
curves, shape of, 98-99, 103

FT Press

FINANCIAL TIMES

In an increasingly competitive world, it is quality
of thinking that gives an edge—an idea that opens new
doors, a technique that solves a problem, or an insight
that simply helps make sense of it all.

We work with leading authors in the various arenas
of business and finance to bring cutting-edge thinking
and best-learning practices to a global market.

It is our goal to create world-class print publications
and electronic products that give readers
knowledge and understanding that can then be
applied, whether studying or at work.

To find out more about our business
products, you can visit us at www.ftpress.com.